At the
KITCHEN
TABLE

At the
KITCHEN
TABLE

The Craft of Cooking at Home

GREG ATKINSON

SASQUATCH BOOKS
SEATTLE

Printed in the United States of America
Published by Sasquatch Books
17 16 15 14 13 12 11   9 8 7 6 5 4 3 2 1

Cover embroidery: Sarah Plein
Cover photograph: Rachelle Longé
Cover design: Anna Goldstein
Interior design and composition: Sarah Plein

Library of Congress Cataloging-in-Publication Data is available.

ISBN-13: 978-1-57061-734-8
ISBN-10: 1-57061-734-1

Sasquatch Books
119 South Main Street, Suite 400
Seattle, WA 98104
(206) 467-4300
www.sasquatchbooks.com
custserv@sasquatchbooks.com

CONTENTS

RECIPE LIST

FOREWORD

BY MOLLY WIZENBERG

Here's the thing: if he wanted to, Greg Atkinson could write a thoroughly chef-y book. He could write about fancy food from the fanciest of restaurant kitchens. He's got the chops to. But he's also got his priorities in order. Though he's been a professional chef for most of his life, he has never lost sight of the place where most of our food, day in and day out, comes from: home kitchens.

I met Greg not all that long ago. He was moderating a panel at a Pike Place Market Foundation event, and I was a panelist. We had been charged with discussing the importance of eating local. (There are tougher jobs, no doubt.) So there we were, sitting around a table of name tags and Sharpies and stale blueberry muffins, introducing ourselves. I felt shy. I had heard Greg on the radio and had read his books and columns, and I asked him what he was working on. He told me about this book, the one you're holding right now. He said it was about home cooking, and then he said something that really struck me. He said it was about the idea that what feeds us is not only the food on the table, but even more, the experience, the *feeling* of sharing a table with the people we care about.

What I love about Greg's cooking, and his writing, is that it's not about extravagant dishes or grand experiences. It's about everyday cooking and eating—albeit, of course, *very good* everyday cooking and eating. It's about a way of living that we all have access to. It's picnics in the winter, homemade school lunches, a fish fry with coworkers. Simple food is the best food, he says, and reading his recipes, it's difficult to argue. I've bookmarked more than half of them.

I'm tempted to say that Greg makes the ordinary feel extraordinary, because he does. But that's not quite it. I hope I'm not putting words in his mouth, but what I think he would rather us feel is that there's nothing extraordinary about eating well and in good company. It's what makes us human. And it's ours for the taking.

ACKNOWLEDGMENTS

This book is filled with the ghosts of people who shaped the world in which I learned to cook.

I am very grateful to those folks who came before me in both my own family and my wife's family, those who helped us appreciate the power of the kitchen table to serve as a focal point for family life. My grandmother, Sabra Quina Sanchez, and my mother, Annie LeClerc Sanchez Atkinson, were always guiding lights to me in the kitchen, as were my father's grandmother, Myrtle Carter Atkinson, and his aunts, Lois Atkinson Geer and Mildred Atkinson Laney, who made amazing meals spring up out of hard ground in all sorts of times. And though he never cooked, my father has always had a deep appreciation for the ritual of the family meal, an appreciation that I inherited along with his love of words. My wife's family has also been an ever-increasing influence on my cooking, and more and more, I find myself cooking and writing to satisfy the tastes and sensibilities of the Lucas clan and the Latourette family.

The book is also filled with tangible evidence of a team of experts at Sasquatch Books who have helped it take shape:

Gary Luke, the ever-patient publisher; Rachelle Longé, the project editor who hammered my essays and recipes into a more readable form; and copy editor Erin Riggio, who makes it look as though I am far more detail-oriented than I really am.

I'm grateful to the faculty and staff at Seattle Culinary Academy, who allowed me to work in their ranks for three years while the recipes for this book took shape. I'm grateful to Kathleen Triesch-Saul and Kathy Andresevic at *The Seattle Times*, who have allowed me for years to formulate ideas for chapters in the form of essays and recipes for *Pacific Northwest* magazine. I'm grateful for early readers of my drafts, including Sharon Ruzumna and Nancy Baggett, who provided helpful insight and good advice when some of the more difficult essays were taking shape. Special thanks go to Emily Young Ventura for testing the pasta recipes and giving me a nudge to jazz them up a little. Most of all I am grateful to my wife, Betsy Lucas Atkinson, and my sons, Henry Lucas Atkinson and William Erich Atkinson, who provide priceless, spontaneous critical evaluations of all my work—both written and cooked—on a routine basis.

INTRODUCTION:
THE ART AND CRAFT
OF COOKING

"What does a chef do? He cooks. And cooking is a craft.
Cooking is repetition. And one must learn the craft."

—THOMAS KELLER

When the arts and crafts movement was launched in the later years of the nineteenth century, it was as much about social reform as it was about design. In England, artists, illustrators, architects, and furniture designers like Walter Crane, John Ruskin, and William Morris, appalled by the industrialized uniformity and low quality of everyday objects, sought to replace the shoddy work that was coming out of factories with handcrafted objects. They believed that such objects would not only improve the quality of life for their users, but would also reinvigorate the crafts and provide meaningful work for artists and craftsmen. In America, craftsmen like Louis Comfort Tiffany, the architects Charles and Henry Greene, and furniture maker Gustav Stickley were motivated by similar ideals. Unfortunately, and somewhat ironically, the objects they produced were too expensive for most folks, and their efforts at egalitarian art became elitist.

At the time of the arts and crafts movement, mass-produced food was still in its infancy, and it probably didn't occur to anyone that the principles of the factory assembly line would eventually come to dominate food production the way they had the manufacture of furniture and decorative items in the home. But today, agribusiness in the form of multinational food giants is responsible for more than 90 percent of what we eat in the developed world. And in much the same way that cheap manufactured goods prompted the arts and crafts movement, the low quality and homogeny of our industrialized food supply has prompted farmers, chefs, and foragers to seek out traditional techniques and ingredients that offer an alternative to the processed grains, meats, and dairy products that constitute the vast majority of modern American foodstuffs. Just as artisans from our grandparents' generation sought to create a better life for craftsmen while producing better goods for the home, food activists now hope to create a better life for farmers and chefs while providing better meals.

So during the first decade of this new century, a burgeoning farm-to-table movement made up of small family farmers, farmers marketers, food writers, and independent restaurant owners has provided for millions of Americans an alternative to the overprocessed and soulless food that left so many of us hungry for something genuine, something with a sense of place to bring to the table at the height of its particular season. But just as the high-quality products of the arts and crafts movement proved too pricey for most people, locally grown food is often perceived as out of reach to most consumers. And while the high and hidden cost of cheap food makes it wildly more expensive in the long run than handcrafted foodstuffs, most people either cannot or choose not to see the impact of agribusiness on the environment and on human health. We continue to shop for mass-produced foods that are loaded with caloric energy but devoid of micronutrients, foods that leave in their wake environmental devastation, compromised human health, and untold animal suffering.

The principles of mass production are especially hard on animals raised for food. When I was an instructor at Seattle Culinary Academy, I taught a class called Sustainable Food Systems. The object of the class was to help students understand where food comes from, to shed some light on how our menu-writing and buying practices impact the world around us, socially, economically, and environmentally. A good deal of the curriculum was devoted to fishing and animal farming. Confronted with what are essentially the atrocities of overfishing, intensive animal agriculture, and concentrated animal feeding operations (CAFOs), many students were saddened, and some were quite upset.

"How do you come to terms with this, Chef?" I was often asked.

"It's difficult," I answered. "I try to balance it with gratitude." On the one hand, I feel a direct, almost spiritual kind of thankfulness to whatever animal gave its life for the flesh that is my meat. But there is more to it than that. I am also grateful to the systems that made this meat or fish available. I am only a generation removed from ancestors who survived the Great Depression and the Dust Bowl. And while my parents, born in the late 1920s, barely remember the Great Depression, their parents, aunts, and uncles begrudgingly shared stories of what it was like to do without, to struggle to get enough to feed their children.

When that generation of Americans came out of the economic devastation of the 1930s and directly into World War II, they did—collectively and individually—whatever they had to do to keep the wheels of industry turning. If the new military industrial food supply system, one modeled after the processes that fed soldiers, had lifted them into the prosperity of the mid-twentieth century, then they wanted to keep it going at any cost.

Most cooks don't want to learn about the horrors of CAFOs in a cookbook; it's just too depressing. And besides, that dark and intriguing topic has already been handled quite well by other writers. It is enough to say, in the words of Robert Martin, director of the Pew Commission on Industrial Farm Animal Production, that "the present system of producing food animals in the United States is not sustainable and presents an unprecedented level of risk to public health and damage to the environment, as well as unnecessary harm to the animals we raise as food."

The good news is that ordinary citizens can change the way things are done. We don't have to sacrifice abundance to reclaim our health, our natural systems, and our dignity. We don't have to give up meat to shut down the CAFOs. We simply have to make better choices about where our meat comes from—and eat less of it. We don't have to give up the diversity of produce we see in our stores; in fact, if we were to shift some of our farming dollars away from commodity crops like corn and soy toward more fruits and vegetables, we could enjoy a greater variety of affordable produce. And if we would just eat more meals in our own homes with our families, we could change the world and have fun doing it.

Mark Hyman, a physician writing for *The Huffington Post*, put it this way: "The extraordinary thing is that we have the ability to move large corporations and create social change by our collective choices. We can reclaim the family dinner, reviving and renewing it. Doing so will help us learn how to find and prepare real food quickly and simply, teach our children by example how to connect, build security, safety, and social skills, meal after meal, day after day, year after year."

In my work as a food journalist and a chef, I have come to know some of the heroes of the contemporary food movement. I've worked with farmers who practice sustainable farming and treat their land and their animals with respect. I have met people who produce outstanding fruits, vegetables, grains, and pulses of unsurpassed quality. I have dipped a toe in waters where shellfish growers work side by side with environmental activists to keep our waterways clean and healthy. And I've met fishermen who practice traditional techniques for drawing a sustainable catch from the sea. Most of all, I have explored myriad techniques developed by home cooks and chefs who take pride in preparing great meals using wholesome ingredients. Practicing this craft of cooking is a deeply rewarding pleasure, and doing it well has implications far beyond our own tables.

Food is so much more than fuel for our bodies. When we purchase and gather food, we empower the people and systems that produced that food to continue, giving tacit approval to their methods. When we cook and eat, we interact in a most intimate way with the stuff that makes up the world in which we live, stuff that eventually becomes part of our own bodies. Oils that make our carrots glisten on the plate, and butter that melts into our toast eventually form the fatty myelin sheaths around the very neural pathways that carry our thoughts and dreams across the mysterious structures of our minds.

Cooking from scratch and eating with family and friends can connect us not only to one another, but also to parts of the world that we might not even be aware of. A pinch of saffron dropped into a pot of stew in my kitchen on a cold, gray day summons up the blue skies of La Mancha. A cake baked in an heirloom pan brings my late grandmother's spirit into my kitchen. And though he lives thousands of miles away, my father joins me for cocktail hour when I choose the right drink and hors d'oeuvres.

The choices we make about what we cook and eat define what it means to be human. When we ignore where our food comes from and how it's prepared, we deny ourselves some understanding of who we really are. If we refuse to consider how our meat was raised, we not only shut our eyes to the grim truth that we are eating the flesh of other animals, but we also deny ourselves a voice in how those animals are treated while they are alive. We fail to participate in the process of determining how farming impacts the land and water, and sooner or later mistakes made in agriculture catch up to us, no matter how hard we try to ignore them. If we don't pay attention, we could lose the food security that previous generations fought so hard to achieve for us.

But if we carefully consider the people, the animals, the land, and the water that produce our food, if we participate to some degree in its preparation and embrace it with all our senses, then we are more fully alive for the effort. I may have spent most of my life working as a professional chef, but in my heart of hearts, I am still a passionate amateur cook, a craftsman in the kitchen.

SPAGHETTI

"The strands of spaghetti were vital, almost alive in my mouth,
and the olive oil was singing with flavor."

—RUTH REICHL

Today's American cook knows that spaghetti is thin pasta to which any number of flavorful additions might be applied. But to those of us who came of age before the last quarter of the American twentieth century, spaghetti was only one thing: long, thin noodles with a sauce made of meat and tomatoes. In fact, for some of us, "spaghetti" had at least as much to do with the sauce as it did with the pasta. Spaghetti sauce was ubiquitous in American homes. A recipe for Easy Italian Spaghetti in the 1965 spiral-bound *Betty Crocker's Dinner in a Dish Cookbook* (which my ironical college-age son gave me for Christmas in 2010) sums up pretty well what most Americans used to expect when spaghetti was for supper.

Ground beef and chopped onion are stirred together in a skillet "until the onion is tender and the beef is browned." An 8-ounce can of tomato sauce and a 10.75-ounce can of "spaghetti sauce with mushrooms" are stirred in along with a teaspoon of sugar, and the whole mess is allowed to simmer for a penurious 5 minutes before it is served over hot cooked spaghetti and sprinkled with grated "sharp American cheese." "Sharp American" here sounds like an oxymoron, but never mind.

My own mother, with her Bolognese heritage, was considerably more generous with the amount of time allotted for the simmering. She usually started the sauce at about three o'clock in the afternoon; this afforded her time to finish any housework and have a nice bath before my father got home from work at around six o'clock; it also gave the meat time to melt into a velvety softness that distinguished her spaghetti sauce from those of my friends' mothers. But unless she had some leftover cooked pork to add to the sauce, which she often did, the basic ingredients of her sauce were not wildly different from Betty's.

Adventurous fans of the Betty Crocker school of cooking could enhance the dish with "Instant-Italy Meatballs," which included a quarter cup of Wheaties or cornflakes; I suppose it hardly mattered which. They were served with "1 pkg. of our noodles Italiano." It seems especially telling that the word "package" had to be abbreviated. It's as if Betty, in her spirited and efficient way, couldn't waste a second writing out the entire word. She, like the homemakers of the era, was presumably too busy.

Somewhere around 1980, this type of spaghetti sauce lost its cache. I hold Marcella Hazan at least partially responsible.

The Classic Italian Cookbook, published that year by Alfred A. Knopf, included five tomato sauces for pasta, and none of them called for ground beef. Bunches of fresh basil and spoons full of olive oil were held out to home cooks, offering them a fresher tomato sauce. A specific variety of tomatoes—the San Marzano—and even a specific grower, one Luigi Vitelli, were mentioned. And, perhaps for the first time, American home cooks began to consider that tomato sauce was not a thing-in-itself, but a variable dish whose flavor might depend on the quality of the ingredients and the skill of the cook. Further mystifying and perhaps thrilling cooks were the formulas for spaghetti dishes that had no tomatoes at all. Spaghetti with garlic and oil was, at least for some of us, a revelation.

But of course it wasn't just Marcella. Those last decades of the twentieth century were rife with new-old Italian dishes. At New York's Le Cirque restaurant, Sirio Maccioni had introduced the world to spaghetti primavera, a jumble of spring vegetables tossed with pine nuts, herbs, and generous amounts of butter and cream; and of course Americans were traveling to Italy themselves and bringing home tales and recipes of simple and delicious dishes that changed forever how they felt about pasta and about life in general.

I was cooking at a small restaurant in a fairly remote corner of Washington State in 1985 when the chef came home from an exploratory trip to Rome and taught me to make the spaghetti carbonara he encountered there, a formula that I learned by eyeballing and weighing ingredients with my hand and only later transcribed with measurements and specific times. That was around the time I first encountered the joy that is fresh basil and learned to make pesto, too. I thought our spaghetti carbonara and our spaghetti with pesto were as good as anything I had ever eaten.

By the time my sons were old enough to have anything to say about it, spaghetti in my own kitchen could mean any number of things. In spring, it would probably be some variation on that Le Cirque–born Italian American pasta primavera. In summer, fresh tomatoes and basil would play a starring role with a nod to Marcella and her reverence for premium ingredients simply prepared. And if we came home from foraging for mushrooms in the fall, a spaghetti dinner might involve chanterelles and cream. In winter, it might be a modified version of the classic carbonara, made with smoked bacon instead of the more bona fide Italian pancetta.

SPAGHETTI PRIMAVERA

According to New York City legend, Tuscan-born restaurateur Sirio Maccioni introduced this dish to friends, including the late New York Times food editor Craig Claiborne, at a casual gathering in the mid-1970s. Claiborne hailed it as the best pasta dish in a quarter of a century. When readers flocked to Maccioni's restaurant, Le Cirque, and found that the dish was not on the menu, Maccioni persuaded his chef to remedy the situation. But Maccioni told multiple stories regarding the origins of this dish, and the butter and cream bear the marks of his French chef, Jean Louis Todeschini. This version is based on something I cooked up in a friend's house in Bolinas, California, when I was on a road trip in the early 1980s. With carrots instead of the more typical tomatoes, I think my version is more springlike than the original.

For the pasta and vegetables

1 gallon water

2 tablespoons kosher salt

1 pound spaghetti

2 cups broccoli florets, cut into 1-inch pieces

2 medium carrots, peeled and cut into matchsticks

2 cups (about ½ pound) snow peas, trimmed and halved
lengthwise, or 1 cup frozen peas

6 fat asparagus stalks, peeled and sliced ¼-inch thick

2 tablespoons olive oil

For the sauce

¼ cup olive oil

⅓ cup pine nuts

½ pound mushrooms, thinly sliced

1 teaspoon finely minced garlic

⅓ cup dry white wine, such as pinot grigio

⅔ cup heavy cream

Kosher salt and freshly ground pepper

For finishing the dish

6 tablespoons unsalted butter, cut into small pieces
⅓ cup finely chopped flat-leaf parsley
⅓ cup finely chopped green onions
1 ½ cups freshly grated Parmesan cheese, divided

◇ To prepare the pasta and vegetables, in a large pot, bring the water and salt to a full, rolling boil and stir in the spaghetti. After about 8 minutes, when the spaghetti is almost done, stir in the broccoli, carrots, snow peas, and asparagus. Cook until the broccoli turns bright green, 1 or 2 minutes. Drain the spaghetti and the vegetables and spread them out on a baking sheet to cool and halt the cooking process. Toss the hot pasta and vegetables with the olive oil to prevent the noodles from sticking together.

◇ To prepare the sauce, in a large sauté pan over medium heat, warm the olive oil. Add the pine nuts and stir until the pine nuts begin to color, about 30 seconds. (Watch closely, as pine nuts go from golden brown to burned in a matter of seconds.) Stir in the mushrooms and garlic and cook for 1 minute more. The mushrooms will release some steam, lower the oil temperature, and prevent the pine nuts from burning. Add the white wine and cook until it is reduced to a glaze around the mushrooms, about 2 minutes. Stir in the cream and increase the heat to high to boil and reduce the cream by about half. After about 2 minutes, toss the pasta and vegetables in with the bubbling sauce and season to taste with salt and pepper.

◇ To finish the dish, swirl in the butter, parsley, green onions, and ¾ cup of the Parmesan cheese. Pass the remaining ¾ cup Parmesan separately. Serve immediately.

Makes 6 servings

SPAGHETTI WITH TOMATOES, GARLIC, AND BASIL

Fresh tomatoes soften beautifully as they are bathed in hot olive oil. And when the olive oil is already inhabited by bright green basil leaves and slices of fresh garlic, the effect is synergistic. Be sure to drop the basil leaves directly into the hot oil before the liquid of the tomatoes cools it down—the intense heat will destroy the enzyme that causes basil leaves to blacken and they will remain bright green. If you want a dish with more punch, add dried red chile flakes, olives, or anchovies to the basic sauce.

1 gallon water

2 tablespoons kosher salt

1 pound spaghetti

¼ cup plus 2 tablespoons extra-virgin olive oil

1 ounce basil leaves

4 cloves garlic, peeled and thinly sliced

1 to 2 teaspoons dried red chile flakes (optional)

1 pound (about 6 medium) Roma tomatoes, cut lengthwise into
½-inch wedges

1 cup chopped green olives (optional)

One 2-ounce tin of anchovies in olive oil (optional)

Kosher salt and freshly ground black pepper

½ cup freshly grated Parmesan cheese, as an accompaniment

◇ In a large pot, bring the water and salt to a full, rolling boil and stir in the spaghetti. Boil the spaghetti until it is barely tender, about 10 minutes, and drain. Spread the pasta out on a baking sheet to cool and halt the cooking process. Toss the pasta with 2 tablespoons of the olive oil to prevent the noodles from sticking together. The pasta may be prepared ahead up to this point and finished later.

◇ Put the remaining ¼ cup of olive oil in a large sauté pan over medium-high heat, and when the oil is hot, drop in the basil leaves. (Make sure they are completely dry or the oil will spatter uncontrollably.) Add the sliced garlic and the chile flakes, and sauté until fragrant, but not browned, about 30 seconds. Add the tomatoes and sauté for 2 minutes, or until the tomatoes are soft and heated through. Add the olives and anchovies, and cook just until heated through, about 2 minutes. Season the sauce to taste with salt and pepper.

◊ Toss the sauce with the cooked pasta until the spaghetti is heated through and the tomatoes are evenly distributed. Serve with the Parmesan cheese passed separately.

Makes 6 servings

SPAGHETTI WITH CHANTERELLES

Modeled after a recipe in Langdon Cook's charming book Fat of the Land, *this dish comes together in minutes. A quick sauté in butter and a generous splash of cream give the chanterelles in this dish a sumptuous quality that turns an ordinary pasta dinner into a feast. The dark meat from a leftover roast chicken has a texture similar to the shards of chanterelles; if you happen to have some leftover roast chicken on hand, this is a great way to incorporate it into a new meal. If you don't have any cooked chicken, enjoy an equally delicious vegetarian version of the dish. Make sure that before you begin boiling your pasta, all your sauce ingredients are prepared; the sauce comes together in the time that it takes your pasta to cook.*

For the noodles

2 quarts water
1 tablespoon kosher salt
½ pound spaghetti

For the mushroom sauce

¼ cup (½ stick) unsalted butter
1 pound fresh chanterelle mushrooms, torn lengthwise into bite-size pieces
1 cup heavy cream
1 teaspoon kosher salt
1 teaspoon freshly ground black pepper
1 teaspoon dried thyme
2 cups cooked chicken thigh meat, torn into bite-size pieces (optional)
1 cup (about 4 ounces) frozen sweet peas, preferably organic

For finishing the dish

2 tablespoons olive oil
1 cup freshly grated Parmesan cheese

◇ In a large pot, bring the water and salt to a full, rolling boil and stir in the spaghetti. Boil the spaghetti until it is barely tender, about 10 minutes.

◇ While the spaghetti is cooking, make the sauce. Melt the butter in a large sauté pan over medium-high heat and cook the mushrooms until they release their water and start to dry out, about 5 minutes. Stir in the cream, salt, pepper, and thyme, and then add the chicken meat and peas. Stir the sauce gently until the chicken and peas are heated through.

◇ Drain the spaghetti noodles and toss them with the olive oil. Toss the sauce with the pasta, then distribute evenly among 4 serving bowls. Top each serving with a generous sprinkling of Parmesan.

Makes 4 servings

SPAGHETTI ALLA CARBONARA

A study in simplicity, this dish derives most of its character from the techniques that bring the simple ingredients together. A little of the cooking water combined with the eggs and the fat from the pancetta and olive oil forms a creamy sauce around the pasta. It is vital that the eggs not be allowed to scramble. A skilled restaurant cook who prepares this dish can usually keep the pasta wet enough and stir quickly enough to add the eggs directly to the cooking pot without allowing them to scramble. But my method is more foolproof: the eggs are whisked into some of the cooled pasta cooking water before they go into the hot bacon-fat mixture.

For the sauce base

4 ounces pancetta, bacon, or guanciale, cut into ¼-inch dice

¼ cup extra-virgin olive oil

4 cloves garlic, peeled and thinly sliced

I tablespoon dried oregano

2 teaspoons dried red chile flakes

For the pasta

I gallon water

2 tablespoons kosher salt

I pound spaghettini (thin spaghetti)

For finishing the dish

4 eggs

I cup grated Pecorino Romano cheese, divided

¼ cup fresh parsley, chopped

◇ To make the sauce base, cook the pancetta with the olive oil in a large saucepan over medium-high heat until the fat is rendered and the bits of pork are lightly browned. Take the pan off the heat and stir in the garlic, oregano, and chile flakes. Allow the mixture to cool to room temperature; the bacon will continue to color as the oil cools.

◇ To cook the pasta, in a large pot, bring the water and salt to a full, rolling boil and stir in the spaghettini. Cook just until the pasta is al dente, about 6 minutes; it should be slightly firm, but when a piece is broken, it should not have a hard white core. Scoop ¾ cup of the cooking water out of the pot and drain the pasta. Allow the reserved cooking water to cool until you can hold the tip of your finger in it without it burning.

◇ To finish the dish, whisk the eggs into the reserved cooled pasta cooking water. Reheat the pork and olive mixture over medium-high heat until the mixture begins to sizzle. Stir in the cooked pasta along with the egg and water mixture, stirring with tongs or a wooden spoon until the eggs begin to thicken the sauce. Do not allow the eggs to scramble. Stir in ¾ cup of the Pecorino Romano and the chopped parsley, and distribute the pasta among 6 warm serving bowls. Top with the remaining ¼ cup grated cheese and serve at once.

Makes 6 servings

A WINTER PICNIC

"I have a weakness for picnics, especially in winter, when the mosquitoes cease from troubling and the ant-hills are at rest."
—ELIZABETH VON ARNIM

Picnics and summer go hand in hand. But anyone can picnic in summer; more creative and adventurous souls picnic in winter, and they're better off for it.

Oh sure, there are drawbacks—inclement weather, a lack of willing companions, frostbite, whatever—but the advantages of picnicking in winter provide more than ample compensation. Consider this: When less hardy souls have shuttered themselves indoors, the most scenic spots are yours and yours alone. There are no bugs to speak of, and any company you manage to coax along is bound to be bold and interesting. What's more, in the cold winter air, everything tastes ten times better than it does in the forced heat of the indoors.

I think my fondness for winter picnics might have been born before I ever experienced one. I was probably ten years old when my widowed grandmother surrendered her home to go and live with one of my aunts, and we came into her books. She had mountains of old novels, and since my grandmother knew that I was a reader, she pointed out works by a few of her favorite writers. She loved the poet Walt Whitman and made sure I had her copy of *Leaves of Grass*. She liked the Victorian novelists E. M. Forster and Elizabeth von Arnim, whose vaguely feminist works included *The Enchanted April*. "You'll like these," promised my grandmother, and I did.

"Yesterday by way of a change," wrote von Arnim in *Elizabeth and Her German Garden*, "we went for a picnic to the shores of the Baltic, ice-bound at this season, and utterly desolate at our nearest point."

I discovered firsthand the joys of eating outdoors in winter some years later when I was cooking at a ski resort. One of the perks was a free lift ticket for the season, so during my breaks and on my days off, I could ski for free. Since I didn't want to waste any time not skiing, I would bring a sandwich and eat it standing on my skis in some sunny spot beside one of the less crowded runs, my cheeks flushed with a combination of windburn and exercise. I thought my sandwiches tasted better in the open air than they did in the crowded lodge.

When I first started dating the girl who would eventually become my wife, I discovered that she, too, had a penchant for taking meals outside in the cold. Raised on ski trips in the Cascades and boating trips in the San Juan Islands, Betsy loves the outdoors. One of our early dates was a short hike the day after Thanksgiving. We were on San Juan Island, and we headed into the woods with turkey sandwiches and a thermos full of hot tea. The leaves crunched under our feet, and chill breezes from the open straits wended their way between the bare branches of the trees around us.

After we were married, we went to live on San Juan for a dozen years, and there, winter picnics became something of a habit. I remember one day in particular, when we were trapped inside for days on end by a nor'easter that put out the power, froze our water pipes, and threatened to drive us insane. I probably would have succumbed, but Betsy packed a lunch, filled a thermos with hot tea, and insisted that we go see Jackle's Lagoon in the ice.

We had a child by then, and I was afraid he would freeze. But Betsy bundled him up and stuffed him into a carrier backpack. "He'll be fine," she insisted. The trail was a study in frost; lacy shrouds crept over fallen leaves and long, spiked rays stabbed along the ground. And the sky, crystal clear that day, felt as if it had been rent open to the absolute emptiness of space. Beside the lagoon, which was frozen into wide gray and white ripples of ice, our woolly mittens stuck to the frozen sandwiches, and the tea threatened to freeze in the cups. But there, with our baby in one pack and the picnic supplies in another, the world seemed new again. As von Arnim wrote, "The stillness of an eternal Sunday lay on the place like a benediction."

And though the baguette sandwiches, oatmeal cookies, and juicy pears were good, the food we ate didn't matter at all. What mattered was that we were in the light and the air— what picnics are really all about.

"It seems to me," wrote Walt Whitman in his poem "The Sleepers," "that every thing in the light and air ought to be happy, / Whoever is not in his coffin and the dark grave let him know he has enough."

BAGUETTE SANDWICHES

Assemble the sandwiches at home, cut into single-portion lengths, and then wrap each portion in parchment paper or waxed paper before heading out to face the elements with a thermos of hot tea, some cookies, and fruit.

> 1 baguette, about 24 inches long
> 4 tablespoons olive oil
> 4 teaspoons red wine vinegar
> Kosher salt and freshly ground black pepper
> Eight 1-ounce slices Swiss or Havarti cheese
> Eight 1-ounce slices cooked turkey or ham (optional)
> 4 large leaves of green leaf lettuce, rinsed and patted dry

◇ Split the baguettes lengthwise. In a small bowl, whisk the oil and vinegar with a fork until well combined, then drizzle the mixture over each open side of the cut bread. Sprinkle the bread with salt and pepper to taste.

◇ Lay the slices of cheese and meat in slightly overlapping shingles down the length of the bottom of the loaf and top with the lettuce leaves. Plant the top of the loaf over the filling and cut each baguette in half.

Makes 4 servings

NEW-FANGLED COWBOY COOKIES

No one seems to know exactly where or when these popular oatmeal chocolate chip cookies originated, but I would be willing to bet they came from Texas. After all, Texas is cowboy country, and the semisweet chocolate, pecans, coconut, and brown sugar suggest the same sort of pantry staples that gave rise to German chocolate cake, an all-American recipe that can be traced to Dallas, Texas, where a homemaker incorporated German's brand chocolate into a coconut-and-pecan-topped chocolate layer cake in the 1950s. Unlike the many versions containing boxed cereals, my cookie is built on a base of mashed dates. I worked these cookies up when I was deeply under the influence of the natural foods movement in the late 1970s, but that doesn't mean they taste at all like so many of the dreadful "health foods" from that era. Soft and chewy with crispy elements and a wealth of textural variations, these might just be the best drop cookies of all time. I often make a batch of the dough, scoop it all out, and bake only a few dozen at a time; extra dough balls keep for a month or two in the freezer.

½ cup chopped dates

¼ cup water

½ cup (1 stick) unsalted butter, at room temperature

½ cup pecan, canola, or corn oil

1 cup granulated sugar

1 cup brown sugar

1 egg

1 teaspoon vanilla

1 cup unbleached all-purpose flour

1 cup whole-wheat flour

1 teaspoon baking soda

½ teaspoon kosher salt

½ teaspoon baking powder

2 cups quick-cooking oats

6 ounces (about 1 cup) finely chopped bittersweet chocolate

6 ounces (about 1 cup) finely chopped milk chocolate
1 cup dried or frozen shredded coconut, preferably unsweetened
1 cup chopped pecans

◇ Preheat the oven to 350°F and line 2 baking sheets with parchment paper.

◇ In a small saucepan over medium-high heat, combine the dates and water. When the water begins to boil, reduce the heat to low and let the dates simmer until they are falling apart, about 5 minutes. Transfer the dates with any remaining cooking liquid to the bowl of a stand mixer and add the butter, oil, sugar, brown sugar, egg, and vanilla. Mix on medium speed until the dates are pureed and the ingredients are well combined, about 2 minutes.

◇ In a separate large mixing bowl, whisk the all-purpose flour, whole-wheat flour, baking soda, salt, and baking powder together. Stir in the oats, bittersweet chocolate, milk chocolate, coconut, and pecans. Transfer the flour mixture into the bowl with the butter, sugar, and egg mixture and mix on low speed just until combined.

◇ Using a 1-ounce scoop or a tablespoon, drop dollops of cookie dough onto the parchment-lined cookie sheets, allowing about 2 inches of space between each cookie.

◇ Bake the cookies on the middle two racks of the oven until the cookies puff up and turn golden brown, about 12 minutes. To ensure that the cookies bake evenly, switch the pans in the oven halfway through baking, placing the top tray on the bottom and vice versa. Cool on racks. Repeat with the remaining cookie dough, or scoop the remaining dough into dollops, freeze on a baking sheet, then transfer to an airtight container and place in the freezer to be baked later.

Makes 60 cookies

ON CYPRESS STREET

"If music be the food of love, play on."

—WILLIAM SHAKESPEARE

One of the greatest influences on my cooking was a woman who seldom cooked when I knew her; she claimed she didn't like to cook at all. "I'd rather do dishes any day," she used to say. "Besides," she reasoned, "I raised seven girls and one son, and they can all cook so I don't have to."

Had she lived a few days longer, my maternal grandmother, Mary Sabra Quina Sanchez, would have been ninety-one. When she died in 1995, she was in her own bed, surrounded by her children, her grandchildren, and her great-grandchildren. My sister was brushing her hair.

Born just three years after Queen Victoria died, when Theodore Roosevelt was president of the United States, Grandma spent her childhood and young adulthood in a country where women couldn't vote. In fact, she spent most of her life in a world that was very different from the one in which she died. Stories of her childhood fascinated me when I was growing up. Vegetables, dairy products, and ice were delivered to her home by horse-drawn cart, a tradition that continued well into her adult life, after my mother was born. Her children grew up listening to the radio, and her grandchildren watched TV, but she spent the evenings of her childhood singing around the piano with her brothers, sisters, and cousins. My great-grandfather thought a piano would mean more to his wife than a diamond, and so my great-grandmother received a piano in lieu of an engagement ring.

"We would just pick out a song and sing it," my grandmother said. "That would remind one of us of another tune and we would plunk away at the piano until we figured that one out, and then we would sing it, too." She might have been happy to know that after her funeral, a group of us stood around my mother's kitchen and sang the old songs for hours.

There was a period in my grandmother's life during the early 1980s when she hardly left her room. Content with her view of the yard outside, and with her solitaire game inside, she gave up shopping and trips to her children's homes because, she said, she was afraid of falling. She may in fact have become afraid of a world that had changed too drastically in her lifetime for her to feel comfortable in it. Psychologists call it agoraphobia, fear of the outdoors, or fear of the marketplace.

Even as a young girl, Grandma didn't like to stray too far from the hearth. Though I never saw her drive a car, she told me once that she learned to drive as a teenager and drove fast and far in an open roadster with her closest sister and two of their friends. Then, suddenly, "I realized that if anything were to happen to that car, I would be stuck out there somewhere with no way to get back, and I got so nervous I had to ask my friend to drive us home." The memory of it made her short of breath. "I decided then and there," she said, "that if I made it back without a flat tire or a breakdown, I would never drive again." She never did drive again.

Personally, I suspect that she may have had private reasons for her self-imposed cloistering. My grandmother was in the habit of making deals with God. She was a devout Catholic, and as far as I could tell, the bulk of her religious observance took the form of self-denial. She gave up ice cream and pie in exchange for God's favors. (She made exceptions for birthday parties, when she would happily eat ice cream, and whenever anyone in the family made pies, we would bake a little of the pie filling in a custard cup so that she could have dessert. She enjoyed lemon meringue custard, pecan custard, and pumpkin custard with no qualms about their similarity to pie.)

So it could be that she gave up leaving the house in some bizarre deal she made with her maker. In any case, after almost a decade of seldom leaving her room, she did eventually begin to travel again. And at every home she visited, she enjoyed foods like pound cake, cheese grits, baked ham, potato salad, and "Aunt Rachel Chicken," a strange dish that my mother and all her sisters made often. Named after my grandmother's sister Rachel, the dish was simply a cut-up chicken baked in bottled Catalina salad dressing. But Grandma also enjoyed all the old-fashioned dishes that captured my imagination when I started to cook "from scratch," abandoning the convenience foods I grew up with in favor of meals built on whole, natural ingredients.

Many of the first dishes I learned to cook were semi-subconscious attempts to appeal to my grandmother's palate. She was a woman who always appreciated good food and noticed every attempt to make it more interesting. She laughed at me when I started volunteering at the food co-op in exchange for wholesale prices on what I bought there. "You're like some kind of hippie," she said. But she appreciated what I cooked with those all-natural ingredients. After decades of eating cakes made from boxed mixes, my grandmother swooned over a fudge marble cake baked with evaporated cane juice, real butter, and organic flour. "Now that's real fudge!" she exclaimed.

After her funeral, after the singing, when her survivors were gathered around the table, still eating and drinking, my parents, aunts, and uncles mused about how it might be for Grandma in heaven. "I think she's at the old Martine's Restaurant and that waiter—what's his name—is bringing out the shrimp rémoulade that your grandfather always ordered," said my father. But I wasn't so sure. I think going out would not have been her first option. She liked to eat at home.

One of the last times I saw her, I walked in on my grandmother when she was napping in her chair. When she awoke and saw me standing there, she gasped and clutched her chest. "You scared me half to death," she said. "I thought you were Phillip Joe." Phillip Joe was my grandfather who died when I was just a year old, leaving Grandma a widow for more years than she had been a wife. She told me that she had been having a recurring dream about him. "When we lived down there on Cypress Street," she told me, "I used to get supper on the stove and then I would take a bath in the afternoon and sit on the porch until he got home." She loved slow-cooked, braised dishes that could tend themselves while she worked a puzzle or relaxed on the porch. "In the dream," she said, "I have already had my bath and put on a clean dress, and I'm sitting on the porch waiting for Phillip Joe. He's just about to turn the corner and I'm leaning forward in my chair so I can see his face," she said, leaning forward in her chair. "And then, just like that, I wake up."

She sat still for a while, looked at me as if she might be finished with the story, then decided to go on. "I know that one night I won't wake up and I'll get to keep on dreaming long enough for him to come on up to the porch and give me a kiss."

That, I suppose, would be heaven for her: an evening safe at home, with supper on the stove and the one she loved nearby.

PERFECT POT ROAST

My grandmother made brilliant pot roast. I never asked her how she did it, but I know part of it had to do with the beef we had back then. It was plain, grass-finished stuff. Nowadays, the government subsidizes corn, so it's cheaper to fatten cattle on expensive grain than it is to finish them naturally on grass. But grass-fed beef is healthier and has a better flavor. Once a year, I buy a quarter of a grass-finished steer from a farmer I trust and turn to old-fashioned dishes like this one to produce the kinds of meals my grandmother would enjoy. The subtle transformation that renders a tough and inexpensive cut of beef into a meltingly tender indulgence can happen only with time. Allow five or six hours to prepare this dish. Only about thirty minutes of that time will be actual hands-on preparation. The bulk of the time is spent doing whatever you want: taking a bath, for example, or waiting on the porch for your lover to come home.

> One 3- to 5-pound chuck roast
> 2 to 3 tablespoons kosher salt, depending on size of the roast
> 1 tablespoon freshly ground black pepper
> 3 tablespoons olive oil
> 1 medium yellow onion, peeled and thinly sliced
> 4 medium carrots, trimmed and cut into ½-inch coins
> 2 stalks celery, thinly sliced
> 4 cloves garlic, peeled and thinly sliced
> 2 tablespoons sugar
> 1 teaspoon dried thyme
> 4 cups chicken or beef stock

◇ Pat the roast dry with paper towels and sprinkle it on both sides with the salt and pepper. Heat the olive oil in a large, heavy-bottomed pot or Dutch oven over medium-high heat. When the oil is quite hot, but not yet smoking, carefully lay the roast in the bottom of the pan and let it brown on one side, about 5 minutes. Turn the roast and brown the other side, about 5 minutes more.

◇ Take the roast out of the pan; you can rest it on the overturned lid. In the fat left behind, sauté the onion, carrot, and celery until the onion is soft and beginning to brown, about 5 minutes. Stir in the garlic, sugar, and thyme and sauté until fragrant, about 1 minute more.

◇ Stir in the stock and bring the liquid to a full, rolling boil. Reduce the heat to low, put the roast back in, cover the pan, and allow the roast to simmer until it is very tender, about 5 hours. Check the roast from time to time to make sure the liquid is still simmering, but if steam pours out from under the lid, the temperature is too hot. The ideal temperature is between 185°F and 200°F (a slow simmer).

◇ When the beef is tender, lift it out of the pot and rest it on the overturned lid, or on a platter. Strain the liquid from the pot into a saucepan, pressing hard on the solids to extract as much liquid as you can. Discard the solids. Boil the strained cooking liquid, uncovered, over high heat until it is reduced to about 2 cups. Put the roast back in the pot and keep it warm until serving time.

Makes 8 to 10 servings

BUTTERY MASHED POTATOES

I usually like to keep things as simple as possible, but when it comes to mashed potatoes, simple is not always best. Especially if you are planning to serve the potatoes with a pot roast that took five hours to prepare, a little extra effort is worthwhile. Instead of battering cooked potatoes with a standard masher, I like to take a moment to push them through a food mill or a potato ricer. It may take a little extra time, but one advantage is that the peels become trapped in the mill, so there is no need to peel the potatoes ahead of time. Plus, all the water-soluble vitamins, minerals, and flavor from those peels will be transferred into the cooked potatoes.

2 pounds (about 4 medium) Yukon Gold potatoes

1 tablespoon kosher salt

¼ cup (½ stick) unsalted butter

◇ Scrub the potatoes thoroughly, but don't peel them, then cut them into 1-inch cubes. Put the cubed potatoes and the salt in a large saucepan and add enough water to cover them with about an inch of water. Cook the potatoes over medium-high heat until they are quite tender and beginning to fall apart, about 15 minutes.

◇ Drain the potatoes, reserving about ½ cup of the cooking liquid. Return the empty saucepan to the stovetop over low heat; place the food mill over the top. Force the potatoes through the mill and whisk in the reserved cooking liquid and the butter.

Makes 6 servings

STEWED ZUCCHINI

One of the only things my grandmother ever taught me to make was a simple dish of stewed vegetables. I dropped in on her at lunchtime one day, and she had prepared a little pot of stewed okra for herself. Though she seldom cooked at that stage of her life, she did occasionally sneak into the kitchen and cook something she wanted to eat. I ate the stewed okra with her and determined it was just about the best thing I had ever eaten. When I asked her how to make it, she patiently described every step of the process and assured me that if I couldn't find okra, I could make it with any vegetable I wanted. Since I have lived most of my life far from okra country, I have used this technique on other vegetables. The technique, which is very similar to making gumbo, works especially well with summer squash. Here, as in gumbo, a roux of flour and oil is the foundation of the dish, but in this case, the roux comes together more quickly; it's just barely browned.

¼ cup corn or canola oil

¼ cup all-purpose flour

½ small onion, peeled and finely chopped

½ green bell pepper, seeded and finely chopped

1 stalk celery, finely chopped

1 teaspoon crushed garlic

½ teaspoon dried thyme

1 teaspoon kosher salt

½ teaspoon freshly ground black pepper

One 14-ounce can chopped tomatoes

1 pound zucchini or yellow squash, trimmed and cut into
  ½-inch slices

◇ To make the roux, combine the oil and flour in a medium saucepan with a heavy base over medium heat, stirring constantly with a wooden spoon until the roux is a light golden brown, about 5 minutes. Watch the roux closely to prevent burning.

◇ Add the onion, bell pepper, and celery and cook until the vegetables are soft, about 5 minutes. Stir in the garlic, thyme, salt, and pepper, then stir in the tomatoes and continue stirring until the mixture is boiling.

◇ Stir in the squash, and when the mixture is boiling again, reduce the heat to low. Cover the saucepan and allow the squash to simmer until it is quite tender, about 30 minutes.

Makes 6 servings

FUDGE MARBLE POUND CAKE

In the early seventies, my mother scored one of those aluminum Bundt cake pans, the American answer to the kugelhopf. *Cake mixes, designed specifically for the pan, were all the rage, but I wanted to bake a cake from scratch. So, armed with Mother's 1-2-3-4 cake recipe (1 cup shortening, 2 cups sugar, 3 cups flour, and 4 eggs), I set out to create a formula for a fudge marble pound cake. Four decades later, I'm still at it. This is the latest manifestation. A loaf pan fills in for the old Bundt pan, butter has replaced the shortening, another egg has been added, and cornstarch replaces some of the flour, but the process is the same. Most important, the spirit of the cake is intact.*

1 cup (2 sticks) unsalted butter, softened to room temperature

1¾ cups sugar

5 eggs, at room temperature

2 teaspoons vanilla extract

2 cups unbleached all-purpose flour

2 tablespoons cornstarch

1 teaspoon baking powder

1 teaspoon kosher salt

½ cup milk, at room temperature

¼ cup brown sugar

¼ cup unsweetened cocoa powder

◇ Rub an 8- or 10-cup Bundt cake pan or a 9-by-5-by-3-inch loaf pan with butter, dust it with flour, and shake out the excess. (Alternatively, you can coat it lightly with nonstick spray.) Preheat the oven to 350°F.

◇ In a large mixing bowl, or the bowl of an electric mixer, whip the butter until it's smooth, then gradually add the sugar, beating all the while, until the mixture is even lighter and fluffier, about 4 minutes. Beat in the eggs, one at a time, beating well after each addition, then stir in the vanilla extract.

◇ In a separate mixing bowl, whisk together the flour, cornstarch, baking powder, and salt. Add the flour mixture in four or five additions to the butter mixture, pouring in a little of the milk with every addition of flour and beating well after each addition.

◇ Transfer all but about 1 cup of the batter to the buttered cake pan. Stir the brown sugar and cocoa powder into the remaining cup of batter and spoon it on top of the batter in the pan. Run a knife through the two batters in a swirling motion to mix them up a little, but do not completely combine them.

◇ Bake the cake in the upper third of the oven until a toothpick comes out clean, about 55 minutes. Allow the cake to cool in the pan for 15 minutes, then transfer it to a rack to cool completely.

Makes 1 cake, serving 8 to 12

FAMILY MEAL

"Keep it simple."
—AUGUSTE ESCOFFIER

Behind the scenes at every great restaurant, cooks make certain meals that customers never see. These are staff meals, family meals, or as the cooks liked to say when I was the chef at Canlis Restaurant in Seattle, "crew chow." By any name, these are the meals that keep the restaurant going. Every restaurant is different and each one has its own policies about feeding the staff, but among better restaurants, a family meal at least once a day is the norm. When I worked at Canlis, there was a staff of about sixty people, and every day at five o'clock we had dinner, and then at eleven or so we shared a substantial evening snack.

Even at the small café in Friday Harbor where I was chef, the entire crew—all six or seven of us—sat down after service every night with bread, wine, and whatever we needed to use up before the next day's service. Mealtime was an opportunity to meet and go over the fine points of service, and a chance to share news of our lives outside the restaurant. We worked and ate together like one big dysfunctional family. Sometimes one of the employees would bring a boyfriend or girlfriend to the family meal, and it was just like bringing home a date to meet the family, only worse. None of us were shy about asking probing personal questions. Still, a good time was generally had by all.

In his book *Kitchen Confidential*, Anthony Bourdain describes the perfunctory family meals presented in the various restaurant kitchens where he worked in New York City. Crew chow in Bourdain's book ranges from the ordinary to the hideous. Most common is the chicken leg, noodles, and salad. Worst is the awful "raft," a mishmash of solids strained out of the stockpot. Most restaurants discard this stuff, but Bourdain insists that at some places, this is all there is for the staff to eat.

When I spent some time in New York as a guest cook, or "stagiére," in three different four-star restaurants, I saw plenty of that famous trinity of chicken, noodles, and salad. But I also saw roast beef, baked fish, deli-style sandwiches, hot dogs—all kinds of ordinary foods that would never have been served in the dining room. All these foods were consumed with gusto by the hungry cooks and waiters. "We eat really good here," said Daniel Boulud's sous-chef, as we served ourselves chicken legs, noodles, and salad, and I had to agree. But the meals in New York's great French restaurants were not quite as interesting as the staff meals in France.

When I worked for a too-brief time at Moulin de Mougins in Provence, then a three-star Michelin restaurant, the family meal gave me an intriguing glimpse into the stratified world of the French restaurant crew. Perhaps it was because my senses were heightened by the excitement of being in a foreign country, or perhaps it was because the food really was extraordinary, but the meals I had there were some of the most memorable crew meals of my life.

Mealtimes at Moulin de Mougins were segregated into three levels of sophistication. The management ate the finest food, almost as good as the food eaten by the guests, and they drank good wine. The waiters and cooks drank modest wine and ate ordinary food. The dishwashers ate mysterious things, pots of lentils and polenta with rejected parts of the animals butchered for the restaurant, and they drank plain, barely fermented wine from collapsible plastic jugs.

On my first afternoon at the restaurant, I was led into the dining room and seated at a table with half a dozen well-dressed sophisticates who were introduced to me as the "direction," or management. I smiled weakly. I was uncomfortable with my French and unable to understand much of what was said.

We were presented with tiny plates of smoked salmon, and I ate as politely as I could while the "direction" practiced obscure idioms in their brilliant native tongue and asked me very slowly if, since I lived in Washington, I lived with the president. "No, no," one of them answered for me, "he's from the West, where they've only just recently chased out the savages." No one spoke a word of English.

I sat quietly as my smoked salmon was exchanged for a neat packet of veal, tied with strings and stuffed with sausage.

My glass was filled with a deep red wine. I struggled with the strings around my veal and glanced nervously at the others who managed to remove their strings with the same fluid ease with which they spoke. My strings wouldn't budge and my tongue would not form a single word in French.

Finally came the cheese course, smooth white Camembert served with bottles of chilled spring water. It was soothing, and I felt fortified enough to look the others in the eye, but I was far too humbled to practice anything I had learned from my French *Jiffy Phrasebook*.

The next day, after shucking two cases of live scallops, I ate with the cooks. We had lambs' brains in browned butter with capers. The meat was pale and soft, and not very appetizing, but the bread and cheese were abundant and so was the wine. Everyone ate quickly so there would be time for cards. The food was pushed aside and out came the deck. The cooks pounded the table with their fists when they lost and stood triumphant with chairs tumbling behind them when they won. I was incapable of following the games.

On the third day, I was assigned to work in the *laboratoire*, a prep kitchen in a separate building behind the main restaurant where all the basic foods were brought in and broken down before they went into the main kitchen. There, whole birds were eviscerated and plucked. Rabbits and deer were butchered. Fresh mushrooms and berries were made into duxelles and sorbets.

In charge of the lab was one of the few honored Master Chefs of France. He was in semiretirement and worked at the restaurant, he said, "just to keep from rotting away." We spent the morning chopping huge bones with an axe on a stump outside the laboratory. Later he would transform them, first into stock and eventually into a rich concentrate known as demi-glace for use by the other chefs. By lunchtime, the stump had been sprayed down with a garden hose and the bones were roasting with aromatic vegetables. We ate from mismatched plates at a bare table in an attic room. With the tattered sleeves of his monogrammed chef's jacket pushed unceremoniously up to his elbows, the grandfatherly chef served spaghetti with meat and tomato sauce. We drank country wine from jelly jars and broke bread directly over the table without bread plates. There was no butter, no cheese, and no pretense. "This, you must understand," he told me instructively in very plain, precise French, "is real food, simple food." I understood every word.

Made with beef from a steer the chef had butchered himself, handmade pork sausage, and fresh tomatoes, the sauce was seasoned unpretentiously with dried herbs, freshly ground pepper, and a sprinkling of commercial chicken bouillon granules. It was the quintessential spaghetti sauce. A gentle wind came through the open windows from the herb garden outside and, more than at any other time since I had been in France, I felt at home. "This is good," I said. "It reminds me of home."

"Of course it does," said the old man as if he knew me, as if he knew my grandmother's kitchen, with its peculiar smells and sounds. "It is real food." Without referring directly to the haute cuisine served in the dining room fifty meters from where we sat, the old master managed to imply that the food served there for hundreds of francs per plate was something less than real. I had come to France to learn the secrets of haute cuisine and learned instead what I had always known: that simple food is the best food.

Most of the best family meals at restaurants are like the best family meals at home: simple, familiar foods served without a lot of fuss or fanfare. People in my crew often cooked the traditional comfort foods they grew up with, and since they came from Laos, Mexico, Japan, and the Philippines, they cooked some pretty interesting crew chow. In addition to great Mexican burritos, Laotian-style pho, and the occasional hamburger, we often had simple treats. I would transform some leftover bread dough into cinnamon rolls, or one of the cooks would whip up a batch of the delectable little Okinawan-style doughnuts known as *andagi*. These were always served at the end of the night when service was over, and knowing they were on the way kept everyone in good spirits, even on the toughest nights.

My favorite staff meal always revolved around chicken adobo, which was prepared almost weekly by my sous-chef, Jeff Taton, who hailed from the Philippines and made the dish as a sort of nod to his own family tradition. Jeff came to work at the restaurant when he was seventeen and continued to work there until he was well into his forties. He served the chicken with steamed rice and salad. Even after eating this dish two or three times a month for more than seven years, I find that it still tastes as good as anything I ever ate in a three-star Michelin restaurant in France. These days I use that same formula to make a pork adobo, which I like even more than the chicken.

TATON'S PORK ADOBO

When we were working together at Seattle's Canlis Restaurant, Jeff Taton made chicken adobo for the crew almost every week. I use the same basic formula to make a pork adobo for my family at home. We buy naturally pastured pork from a family farm—half a pig at a time—and so we're always looking for good ways to cook it. One of the more interesting cuts is something called "country-style ribs," which aren't really ribs at all: they're rectangular pieces of fatty shoulder meat, perfect for a slow braise or a classic Pacific-style adobo. Vinegar is an essential element of this dish, so seek out a good-tasting palm or cane vinegar from an Asian grocery. If neither one is available, rice vinegar may be substituted.

4 pounds country-style ribs

2 tablespoons lard or corn oil

2 cups soy sauce

2 cups palm, cane, or rice vinegar

2 cups water

6 cloves garlic, peeled and crushed

1 tablespoon cracked black peppercorns

2 bay leaves

Steamed white rice, for serving

◇ Pat the ribs dry with a paper towel. Heat the lard in a large Dutch oven, or any heavy stew pot with a tight-fitting lid, over medium-high heat. When the fat is hot, sear the ribs on all sides until they are well browned, about 4 minutes on each side. If the pot is not large enough to accommodate the ribs in a single layer, brown them in batches; when they are all browned, return them to the pan.

◇ Pour in the soy sauce, vinegar, water, garlic, pepper, and bay leaves. Bring the mixture to a boil, then reduce the heat to medium-low. Cover the pan and allow the pork to simmer gently until it is very tender, about 3 hours. Serve spooned over the rice.

Makes 6 to 8 servings

OKINAWAN DOUGHNUTS

Crispy on the outside, moist and cakelike on the inside, these simple doughnuts from Okinawa are popular in Hawaii, where the fried balls of dough are called andagi, *short for* sata andagi, *which roughly translates as "fried sweet." When Okinawan Hawaiian chef Rocky Toguchi was at the helm, they were a popular treat among the staff at Canlis.When I left the restaurant, I started making them at home.*

¾ cup powdered sugar, for coating the doughnuts (optional)

3 cups corn or canola oil, for deep-frying

I egg

½ cup sugar

½ cup milk

I teaspoon vanilla

I cup plus 2 tablespoons unbleached all-purpose flour

2 teaspoons baking powder

½ teaspoon kosher salt

⅛ teaspoon nutmeg

◇ Preheat the oven to 225°F. Line a baking sheet with a large brown paper bag and place in the warm oven. If you want to give the doughnuts a sugar coating after frying, put the powdered sugar in a small paper bag.

◇ If you have a small deep-fryer, use it according to the manufacturer's suggestions. Otherwise, heat at least 3 inches of oil in a deep, heavy stockpot over medium-high heat until a candy thermometer registers 375°F, or until a cube of bread dropped into the oil rises immediately to the surface and becomes golden brown in 1 minute.

◇ In a large bowl, beat the eggs with the sugar until the eggs are well blended and the sugar is almost dissolved, about 1 minute. Stir in the milk and vanilla.

◇ In a separate large bowl, whisk together the flour, baking powder, salt, and nutmeg until combined.

◇ Add the egg mixture all at once to the flour mixture and stir just until the dry ingredients are moistened.

◇ Use a tablespoon or a small (½-ounce) scoop to drop rounds of dough into the hot oil. Fry no more than 5 or 6 doughnuts at a time; crowding the pan prevents the doughnuts from cooking properly. Fry until the doughnuts rise to the surface and roll themselves over, about 4 minutes. (If they doughnuts do not flip on their own, coax them with a fork after about 2 minutes.) They should be golden brown on both sides.

◇ Lift the doughnuts from the oil with a slotted spoon and drain them on the preheated, paper-lined baking sheet. Keep the doughnuts warm while you prepare succeeding batches. Just before serving, shake the doughnuts in the bag of powdered sugar.

Makes 18 small doughnuts

THE ART OF EATING

"Life is what happens to you while you're busy making other plans."
—JOHN LENNON

Cooking at home for ourselves and for our families, we don't usually employ elaborate techniques, but with small flourishes here and references to shared experiences there, we regularly summon emotional responses from our fellow diners. The simplest comfort foods, assembled from the most familiar ingredients, are often more about their aesthetic appeal—how they make us feel—than they are about any function they serve. Even when we feel that cooking has become so rote as to be mindless, the experience of preparing, serving, and eating can become a kind of art.

Perhaps no one expressed this better than Mary Frances Kennedy Fisher, whose evocative prose prompted any number of chefs and cooks from my generation to seek out better ingredients, to open restaurants, and to write cook-books. Moreover, her writings taught us that wherever we were, be it the South of France or the dry hills of Central California, we could summon up something magical with a few slices of a tangerine left to dry on the radiator, or a peach pie shared with loved ones in the open air.

What moved me about her writing and her cooking, and what prompted me to seek her out as a mentor and friend when she was approaching the end of her life, was the simplicity of her approach. That simplicity may have been illusory—she might have toiled over her pages and her pans—but the work never showed. What came through was the artistry. Her recipes read as if they just happened. "From there on," she writes in a recipe for white bread, "when you first assemble the ingredients, the dance begins."

My dance with M. F. K. began when I wrote to her in care of her publisher, expressing my admiration for her work; her response was that I should come and meet her. Barreling down Interstate 5 with our baby in a car seat and a cooler full of food in the back, my wife and I imagined that meeting Fisher might be a gateway to some new life for us.

I imagined that if I met this great writer, cooked for her, and sat at the table with her, some of her glory might reflect onto me, and my life and work would be great too. Maybe, once she read my work, she would recommend me to her editor and then opportunities would unfurl like a great magic carpet before us. The considerable anxiety I felt about being a new father, and my struggles to support our young family would ease up, eventually becoming nothing more than fodder for the wonderful stories I would tell in the future.

I had begun to write essays about cooking and eating for the local paper in the small San Juan Island town of Friday Harbor, and maybe the praise I received from readers had gone to my head. I began to imagine that I was not merely a good cook and a steadfast journalist, but an important food writer. Every week, I paid attention to what we ate. I took mental notes on where we went to gather apples; I logged trips to the dock where I collected spot prawns and Dungeness crabs for the restaurant. I analyzed how it felt to fold ground hazelnuts and whipped egg whites into a "batter" of melted chocolate and butter when I baked a flourless chocolate cake. When I was cooking and collecting food for cooking, I was paying profound attention to what was happening because I knew that when my day off rolled around, I would gather those thoughts and feelings and construct a story that would segue into a recipe for my weekly column.

So even as I was living those moments, honing all five senses to pay attention, to be in the moment with whatever I was doing in the kitchen, I was dwelling in an imaginary future. In that future, I would derive great satisfaction from my "real art"—the essays and books I would craft using these everyday experiences as raw materials. I think that to some degree I missed the point that what I was doing then and there was art. It wasn't the *stories* I wrote about gathering wild rose petals and transforming them into ice cream that mattered. It was gathering the petals; it was the ice cream *itself* that mattered. Or maybe it was both.

At work, I focused on mastering the techniques of the kitchen. In the afternoon, I was roasting and boning ducks, making stock from the bones, and reducing the stock over heat to concentrate its essence into a foundation for the sauce that

I would later ladle over the crisp skin of the duck we served at the restaurant. At home the next morning, I would codify the process of roasting the duck and making sauce from its bones so that I could sell a story about it. Eventually, I thought I would write about cooking full time, and I would not have to actually cook professionally anymore. And yet, cooking was mesmerizing: I was compelled to become intimate with the anatomy of the birds I was cutting up. I became filled with visceral delight as I inhaled the aroma of their roasting, and spellbound when the stock reached a point of concentration that would cause it to thicken and coat the back of a spoon like a shimmering varnish.

Part of being human, I think, is to transcend everyday experience and observe it from a place of detachment. But ironically, that place of detachment can be reached only by delving fully into whatever task is at hand. Cooking daily, and observing myself cooking so that I could write about it later, afforded me that detachment that borders on transcendence. It was a kind of yoga of the kitchen. In the sense that yoga is the yoke that binds the oxen to the plow, cooking kept me connected to the physical world; it harnessed my mind to the work table where my knife was cutting ribbons of sorrel leaves or julienne strips of carrots for the evening's dinner service. Mastery of cooking—becoming so proficient at those tasks that I could do them without thinking—was my meditation.

But the kitchen is no yoga studio. Interruptions are myriad and dangers abound. Knives flash, flames blaze, and hot metal and hot tempers are juxtaposed against cool intervals when lettuce is washed and cold fish are filleted.

I imagined that meeting M. F. K. Fisher would mark a shift from this chapter of my life. So I went to see her. I cooked in her kitchen, ate with her at her table, and read my stories to her. In a way, the visit did change our lives, but not in the way we had expected.

"Mi casa, su casa!" cried Mary Frances from her wheelchair as we tumbled into her house with our cooler full of food and our babe and his diaper bag in our arms. "I'm so glad you've come," she said. "I don't do a lot of entertaining anymore."

As our long day with her unfolded, we came to realize that our visit was something of a strain on Mary Frances, who had Parkinson's disease, but that she was genuinely glad we were there. She lay on her bed and had me read to her from the columns I had written for my local paper. She inserted witty comments and helpful criticisms. For a while, she held my infant son against her chest; he slept while I read. She asked about my life and shared details about her own.

As evening fell and the frogs outside the house began to sing, my wife nursed the baby while I cooked in Fisher's kitchen. Then we steered Fisher's wheelchair across the black tile floor from her bedroom while she pointed out an ancient painting of a woman she called "Sister Age." She flipped the page in a coffee-table book filled with paper cutouts by Henri Matisse as we wheeled her by it. My wife set the table and poured her a glass of wine to go with the oysters we had carted from San Juan Island to California.

"It must have been thrilling to have so much success with your writing," I said to Mary Frances, "all the books, and the articles for *The New Yorker* and *Gourmet*."

"It was thrilling, I suppose," she said, clutching the stem of the wineglass with both hands, straining to make her voice audible. "But all I could think of while I was selling those stories was paying the dentist bills and buying shoes for my daughters. I was writing and writing just to make ends meet, and they never did, you know—ends never met." She looked at me and pursed her red-painted lips with a certain determination.

"But when you're a born writer, and I think you are," she said pointedly, her painted eyebrows measuring my response, "you have to write. It's a compulsion."

So meeting this great food writer was a wake-up call. Her frank views on the writing life made me realize that in all likelihood, I would continue to cook in restaurants to support my family. After all, writing seldom makes one rich. But the time I spent with her also forged a resolve in me that I would continue to write professionally for as long as my mind and body would hold out. Cooking and writing: both of these crafts would be my destiny.

And in the years since that meeting, when I read Fisher's beautiful prose, I think about what Mary Frances taught us— my generation of food lovers—that cooking could connect us to the world. Her writing seemed to imply that through some sensory alchemy, food could link us to remembered times and places. Gathering heirloom products in our kitchens and preparing them according to time-honored techniques would prompt us to preserve and reclaim the environment that produced those foods and the techniques that made it possible to bring them to the table.

Cooking and eating can connect us to the past, to our families and friends, and to environmental issues. What's more, cooking and eating with the attentive eye of someone dedicated to the craft connects us to the sacred present, where it all happens.

In her book *The Gastronomical Me*, M. F. K. Fisher mentions a dish she made in Paris of cauliflower baked with cream and cheese, saying that she could never re-create it to her satisfaction when she was back in California.

"I could concoct a good dish," she wrote, "but it was never so innocent, so simple . . . where was the crisp bread, where the honest wine? And where were our young uncomplicated hungers, too?"

Perhaps the hungers of my generation were never uncomplicated. We were so stuffed with bad bread and dishonest wine that it took considerable effort to banish our mid-twentieth-century malaise and find a good tight head of organic cauliflower and a half-pint of organic heavy cream. But, armed with Fisher's prose, and thanks to the efforts of some heroic farmers, cooks of my generation did eventually find ways to re-create some of M. F. K. Fisher's dishes and to create some new ones of our own.

When I was cooking and writing on San Juan Island, my wife transformed an old cable spool into a garden table, and she surrounded it with mismatched chairs in a spot where we could look out over the other islands and take in the snow-capped peaks of the Cascade Mountains beyond. There we used to serve a casserole inspired by Mary Frances's memories. It was made with cauliflower from the local farmers market and a pint of organic cream. Even today, in my garden on Bainbridge Island, I've served that dish any number of times with a crusty loaf of bread, either homemade or from one of the artisan bakeries that proliferate now. Every time I make it, I think of Fisher and her efforts to celebrate life at the table on its own terms. But it's not nostalgia for the past or remembering M. F. K. that makes me smile when I raise my glass—it's love for the present, this precious incomparable time we call now.

HOMEMADE ARTISAN BREAD

Like every passionate cook I know, I've tried my hand any number of times at making the elusive, crusty artisanal country bread loaf that was impossible to find when I was growing up in the American suburbs in the 1960s. I tried methods of baking loaves that took days on end; I even started a batch of my own sourdough with wild yeast from grape leaves. But nothing really worked until, in November of 2006, Mark Bittman wrote about Jim Lahey from the Sullivan Street Bakery and gave away his formula for no-knead bread. The key to this bread isn't capturing yeast from the wild to make a sourdough starter or buying an expensive clay baking stone for the oven. The secret to artisan-type bread, it turns out, is making a very moist dough with a very small amount of yeast and giving it plenty of time to mature. Lahey's basic bread recipe has appeared in newspapers, magazines, and books with all sorts of variations—beer in place of water, whole wheat in place of white flour. But the technique is always recognizable, and what follows is my own version of this new American classic.

2 cups bread flour

1 cup whole wheat flour

¼ teaspoon active dry yeast, such as Fleischmann's or SAF-Instant

1 scant tablespoon kosher salt

1 ½ cups plus 2 tablespoons water, at room temperature

◇ In a large mixing bowl, combine the flour, yeast, and salt. Stir in the water until blended, cover the bowl with plastic wrap, and allow the dough to rest at room temperature for at least 12 hours, or for as long as 18 hours. The dough will double in size and the surface should be covered with small bubbles.

◇ Cut a 12-inch square of parchment paper and sprinkle it generously with flour. Turn the dough out of the bowl onto a floured work surface and fold it lightly over on itself, coating it with just enough flour to make it barely manageable. Shape the dough into a ball, tucking any seams underneath. Place the dough seam-side down on the floured parchment, transfer the dough and parchment back into the mixing bowl, cover the bowl with plastic wrap, and allow the loaf to rise for about 2 hours. The dough is ready for baking when it has almost doubled in size and a finger pressed into the top leaves an impression.

◇ About 30 minutes before baking, preheat the oven to 450°F. Place a heavy, preferably cast-iron, Dutch oven or stew pot in the oven to preheat. Transfer the dough on the parchment paper into the preheated Dutch oven and cover. Promptly close the oven and bake the loaf for 30 minutes. Uncover and bake the loaf until it is well browned and sounds hollow when tapped, about 20 minutes more. Cool on a rack before slicing.

Makes 1 large 24-ounce loaf

CAULIFLOWER GRATIN

Drawing from Fisher's spare description of this dish, Sunset *magazine published a recipe for "M. F. K. Fisher Memorial Cauliflower Casserole" that achieved a life of its own on the Web and spawned several similar dishes. I have modified the technique and the ingredients over the many years I have been making it. When I followed Fisher's instructions exactly, the elements never really came together; the cheese separated from the cream and failed to cling to the cauliflower. So I now save some of the water in which the cauliflower was cooked to make a simple velouté, which holds the cheese and cauliflower together. Mary Frances might have pooh-poohed my version as unnecessarily complicated, but it seems just right to me.*

2 cups water

1 tablespoon kosher salt

1 small head cauliflower (about 2 pounds), cut into florets

2 tablespoons unsalted butter, plus additional for greasing the pan

2 tablespoons flour

¾ cup heavy cream

6 ounces (about 1 ½ cups) grated Gruyère cheese, divided

½ teaspoon freshly ground black pepper

◇ Preheat the oven to 375°F and butter a 6-cup ceramic gratin dish or a 9-inch square glass baking dish.

◇ In a large saucepan over high heat, bring the water and salt to a boil. Add the cauliflower and cook just until it has lost its raw look and becomes barely fork tender, about 3 minutes. Drain the cauliflower and reserve 1 cup of the cooking liquid.

◇ Over medium heat, melt the butter in the empty saucepan and whisk in the flour. Whisk in the reserved cauliflower cooking liquid, and when the sauce comes to a boil, stir in the cream. Reduce the heat to low and stir in half of the Gruyère and the pepper.

◇ Pile the cauliflower into the buttered baking dish. Pour the sauce over the cauliflower and sprinkle the remaining cheese on top. Bake until the cauliflower is tender and the cheese is browned and bubbling, about 15 minutes. Serve hot with Homemade Artisan Bread and a salad.

Makes 4 servings

A FINE GREEN SALAD

I used to grow a variety of black-seeded green leaf lettuce that made the most wonderful salads. In recent years, I have been less diligent in my efforts at gardening, and I have been forced to rely on whatever I can buy at the market, but the memory of that stuff from the garden is so profound that sometimes I can taste it even when I am eating some other lettuce. I love a simple salad made with a single green, especially when it's dressed in a classic French vinaigrette like the one M. F. K. Fisher describes in The Cooking of Provincial France.

When Fisher was writing, it was almost impossible to find good domestic olive oil, so Americans had to rely on imports. Today, the cost of imported olive oil has risen, and innovative growing techniques have made it possible for California growers to compete with producers in Italy and Spain. Look for quality extra-virgin olive oil from California in large supermarkets and specialty shops, or search for it online. Some growers will even allow you to pre-order oil before it's pressed and bottled so you get the freshest, greenest oil imaginable.

I head green leaf lettuce

I shallot, finely chopped

I tablespoon Dijon mustard

I tablespoon red wine vinegar

6 tablespoons fruity green olive oil, such as California Olive Ranch

Kosher salt and freshly ground black pepper

◇ Pull the leaves off the head of lettuce, allowing them to fall into a clean sink filled with cold water. Swish the leaves around to loosen any soil, then lift the leaves out of the water, leaving any soil behind. Transfer the washed leaves to a salad spinner, or if no salad spinner is available, pile the leaves into one of those mesh bags in which onions are sold. Crank the spinner or take the mesh bag outside and spin it over your head to release any water clinging to the leaves. Transfer the washed leaves to the refrigerator to chill for at least 30 minutes before serving.

◇ To make the vinaigrette, whisk the shallot, mustard, and vinegar in the bottom of a salad bowl until the mixture is completely and thoroughly combined. Add the first tablespoon of oil, a few drops at a time, making sure it is thoroughly incorporated between each addition. Stream in the remaining oil 1 tablespoon at a time, whisking constantly to create a smooth emulsion.

◇ At serving time, tear the salad greens into bite-size pieces and toss them with the dressing. Sprinkle with salt and pepper to taste.

Makes 4 servings

RUBY RED GRAPEFRUIT SORBET

Red grapefruits are one of my favorite fruits, and this sorbet, which I learned to make from the chef at a restaurant where I worked in Friday Harbor in the 1980s, is my all-time favorite way to eat them. Campari is a bitter Italian liqueur usually served as an aperitivo. *It's also one of the essential ingredients in a Negroni cocktail, composed of equal parts gin, red vermouth, and Campari. We sometimes make a variation on that drink in which we replace the vermouth with Ruby Red grapefruit juice; but that's another story.*

> 4 large red grapefruits
> ¾ cup sugar, preferably organic evaporated cane juice
> ¼ cup Campari

◊ Grate 1 tablespoon of the colorful outer rind from one of the grapefruits, then squeeze out all their juice.

◊ Measure the juice. If you have more than 4 cups, use the extra juice for some other purpose. If you have less than 4 cups, add water to make a total of 4 cups of liquid.

◊ Put ½ cup of the grapefruit juice and the sugar in a small saucepan over high heat and stir until the sugar is dissolved; add this syrup to the remaining juice along with the Campari.

◊ Freeze the mixture in an ice cream maker, then transfer it to an airtight container and allow it to firm up in the freezer for 1 hour before serving.

Makes about 1 quart, or 6 servings

THE SUMMER SOLSTICE

"Time is a jet plane, it moves too fast."
—BOB DYLAN

The phone rings and I run inside, kicking off my garden clogs and pulling off my dirt-caked garden gloves to pick it up.

"What are you doing?" our friend Kayla wants to know. Kayla grew up with my wife, Betsy. She went away to school, became an actress, married, had kids, settled in Vermont, trained to be a yoga instructor, and moved back to Washington. But when they are together, Betsy and Kayla are girls again; the years that separate them from their teenage selves evaporate, and whenever we have an opportunity to get together with Kayla and her husband, Michael, Betsy and I jump at the chance.

"What are we doing?" What are we ever doing on a sunny afternoon in June? The summer solstice makes these afternoons seem impossibly, luxuriously long. We're mowing the lawn, weeding a flower bed, thinning the rhubarb, and thinking about pie. "Oh, I don't know," I admit dreamily. "Nothing. Yard work."

"Well, we were thinking you guys should come join us at Mom and Dad's house; we're going to take a walk around the point and grill some salmon."

Kayla's parents live on the south end of Bainbridge Island in a grand old place built in the 1930s by Norwegian craftsmen who found themselves far from home and eager for work during the Great Depression. Hundreds of hours of labor went into the sod roof with its English daisies, the greenhouse-turned-dining room with its indoor Concord grapevine, and the decorative painting that climbs the door-frames, unfurls over the cabinet doors, and tumbles like bind-weed over the outlines of every handcrafted room.

Even better than the house is the enchanted setting. Restoration Point juts into Elliott Bay like the bow of some great ocean liner made of stone, commanding a view of Seattle like no other. Mount Rainier spreads its foothills to the south, and on a clear day, Mount Baker lifts its chin at the northern end of the horizon and does a little pas de deux with Rainier. Wild Nootka roses line the paths to the beach, and a swimming pool perched above the rocky shore beckons to those inclined to take a quick cool dip.

On that sunny afternoon, there is nowhere in the world we'd rather be. I quickly harvest some of the rhubarb I'd been thinning and throw together some flour, butter, and sugar to transform it into a crisp once we get to Restoration Point. I bag a loaf of bread I baked that morning and grab a bottle of wine; then we round up the boys and we're off. The house is only ten minutes from ours, but it feels a world away, and for a few hours after we arrive, we're lost in time, enjoying the simple pleasure of being together; then someone looks at a watch and no one can believe it's after eight o'clock. Every year, when the summer solstice rolls around, and the sun bears down on the Tropic of Cancer, it's as if it never happened before. We can't believe it stayed light this late.

For a few minutes, preparations for the casual supper take on an air of urgency. The salmon goes on the grill, greens from Kayla's garden get sautéed or find their way into the salad bowl, and the rhubarb crisp goes into the oven. Grilled salmon doesn't need much in the way of accompaniments so no one worries about preparing rice or potatoes. For the boys, who always crave extra carbs, we pass the loaf of bread at the table.

Then, before we know it, the light is fading into a Maxfield Parrish–blue-colored sky. Stars begin to shine, and in the fir trees, owls call one another to the hunt. It's as if the years are flying by, and though they were mere boys when we arrived a few hours ago, our sons are suddenly young men, and though we were young adults when the evening began, we are middle-aged folks by the time the sun goes down. The dawn of summer has come and gone.

GRILLED SALMON ON A BED OF MUSTARD GREENS

Heating mustard seeds causes them to pop like popcorn, so beware when they are added to the hot oil. As soon as the greens are added, the popping stops. Like spinach, mustard greens cook down considerably, so what initially looks like a large amount will actually be just enough.

For the mustard greens

1 large bunch (about 1 pound) mustard greens
3 tablespoons olive oil
1 tablespoon whole brown mustard seeds
1 teaspoon kosher salt

For the salmon

Six 6-ounce fillets wild king salmon
2 teaspoons kosher salt
1 teaspoon freshly ground black pepper
2 tablespoons light olive oil or corn oil, plus more for the grill

◇ Start a fire of hardwood or charcoal in an outdoor grill and allow to burn until the wood or coal is fully ignited and partially covered with a layer of white ash, about 30 minutes. Spread the embers or coals into an even layer, and about 5 minutes before you plan to grill the fish, position the grate about 4 inches above the bed of glowing coals.

◇ Prepare the mustard greens. Rinse them and shake off the water. Arrange the leaves in a neat stack and roll the stack into a bundle. Lay the bundle on your cutting board and cut across the bundle with a rocking motion of the knife to cut across the central vein, creating thin ribbon-like strips. Put the cut greens near the stove, along with the olive oil, mustard seeds, and salt, to be sautéed just before the salmon is ready to serve.

◇ Prepare the salmon. Wipe the grill with a cloth dipped in olive oil. Sprinkle the fillets with the salt and pepper and rub them with the olive oil. Place the fillets, skin side up, onto the grill and allow them to broil for 5 minutes. If the oil ignites, extinguish the flames with a little water splashed from a cup or streamed from a squirt gun. With a long spatula, turn the fillets and allow them to broil for 5 minutes more.

◇ As soon as the salmon has been turned, sauté the greens. Put the oil in a sauté pan over medium-high heat and when the oil is smoking hot, add the mustard seeds. They will start to pop. Immediately add the cut mustard greens and the popping will settle down. Move the greens around the pan with a pair of tongs and sprinkle them with the salt. As soon as the mustard greens are wilted and heated through, distribute them evenly among 4 plates. Arrange the grilled salmon fillets on top of the sautéed mustard greens and serve at once.

Makes 4 servings

RHUBARB CRISP

*This recipe is a variation on Willie's Crisp, a Northwest favorite origi-
nally developed by my friend and fellow cookbook author Sharon Kramis,
who told me that one of her students, a certain young man named Willie
Parks, came up with the technique when he was a child. This recipe has
a little more sugar than most formulas for this style of dessert, and it
employs a very unusual way of combining the ingredients that ensures a
very crisp topping. (I have written about the crisp a number of times over
the years, and I once received an e-mail from Eleanor Brekke, who let me
know quite happily that she was married to Willie of Willie's Crisp fame.
Apparently, Willie still makes the crisp and routinely stocks his freezer
with hundreds of pounds of fruit so they always have it on hand.)*

*This makes a lot of crisp for a dessert, perfect if you have a good-size
gathering, but far too much for a small group. Leftovers, served with a
generous dollop of plain yogurt, are great for breakfast.*

> 3 pounds rhubarb, trimmed and cut into ½-inch slices
> 2 cups sugar, divided
> 1 cup unbleached all-purpose flour
> 1 teaspoon baking powder
> ½ teaspoon kosher salt
> 1 egg, lightly beaten
> ½ cup unsalted butter, melted

◇ Preheat the oven to 375°F. Butter a 2-quart glass or ceramic baking dish or eight 6-ounce baking dishes.

◇ In a dry large saucepan over medium-high heat, cook the rhubarb with 1 cup of the sugar, stirring constantly, for about 5
minutes. The sugar will melt into the juices from the rhubarb
and the rhubarb will begin to soften. Transfer the rhubarb to the
prepared baking dish.

◇ In a mixing bowl, combine the flour, baking powder, salt, and
remaining 1 cup of sugar. Add the egg and stir until the mixture
is crumbly.

◇ Distribute the topping mixture evenly over the surface of the cooked rhubarb, drizzle the melted butter over the top, and bake until the fruit is bubbling up around the edges of the baking dish and the topping is very crisp and brown, 35 to 40 minutes for the large pan, about 25 or 30 minutes for the individual baking dishes.

Makes 8 servings

THE FISH FRY

*"Fish, like eggs, should be cooked quickly and lightly, and
served at once in its own odorous heat."*

—M. F. K. FISHER

Not long after I was drafted to become the executive chef
at Canlis, a grand old restaurant in Seattle, I discovered
that Alice Canlis, who married the heir to the family business, grew up in my hometown. If we'd both been born and
raised somewhere nearby, that might not have been much of
a coincidence. But we're both from Pensacola, Florida. After
twenty years in Washington, Alice was the first person I'd met
who came from Pensacola. Discovering that we were both
from that other world made us feel like expatriates finding
one another by chance in a foreign country, or like siblings,
separated in early childhood, rediscovering one another for
the first time as adults.

This understanding of where we come from created a bond between us and made us available to one another in times of family crisis. When my brother died unexpectedly, Alice happened to be in Pensacola visiting her parents, and she and her husband, Chris, were able to come to the funeral. I was comforted by their presence. When Alice's mother was facing the prospect of a long illness that would eventually take her life, I took time out of a visit with my parents to see Alice's mom in the hospital. Alice's mother, also named Alice, was in some ways a lot like Pensacola itself—beautiful, warm, and friendly—and she faced her mortality with aplomb.

I'll never forget walking into her hospital room with my meager little bundle of flowers purchased in haste from a nearby Winn-Dixie supermarket. She was propped up in her hospital bed wearing a white cotton bed jacket. Her husband, Chapman, was seated in a chair near the bed. They didn't see me come in. They weren't talking or watching TV, but neither were they gloomy in their silence—just quiet. The Florida sunlight streamed in through the windows and a peaceful stillness surrounded them. I tapped gingerly on the open door. They both looked slowly my way, smiling.

"I'm Greg," I said, "from Canlis."

"You sure are," said Alice in a slow, dreamy way. I gave her the flowers, and she told me about the kind of meals they were feeding her at the new retirement home. She wished they could be more like what I cooked at Canlis, but they were good, she said. The cadence of her voice reminded me of my grandmother's voice, and the stillness of that hospital room took me back to another era when life was slower and things seemed simpler. We had only a few minutes together, and it was the last time I ever saw her. Whenever I think of her now,

I see her turning slowly toward me with that sweet, expectant smile on her face.

Not long after his wife died, eighty-year-old Chapman came to spend some time with Chris and Alice in Seattle. He wanted to do a fish fry for the Canlis crew. He had done these things for groups ranging from a few dozen up to two thousand. He'd hosted fish fries for politicians, school reunions, and military socials. As it turned out, I was scheduled to be somewhere else on the day of the fish fry, but I spent the day before helping him get ready, and I vowed that the following year, I'd be there to help him. By the following year, the Canlis family had moved out of their lakefront home and into a condominium downtown. So we held the fish fry at my house on Bainbridge Island.

The day before the fish fry, we baked bread and made potato salad, coleslaw, fruit salad, and the filling and topping for a blackberry cobbler. We made the custard base for homemade ice cream and we peeled and deveined dozens of shrimp. Finally, we trimmed and cleaned the rockfish fillets and stacked them in layers of ice in a cooler. Chapman was extremely particular about how each element of his fish fry came together. It was hard for me to stay within the narrow confines of his directives, but worth the effort.

It was more than just the recipes that made Chapman's Pensacola-style fish fry unique; there were techniques and rituals that set a pace and a mood for the party. Before any fish was fried, all the other food was prepared and put out on a big buffet table, accessible from both sides. "People have to be able to get at it," explained Chapman. Also, before any fish was allowed to touch the oil, hush puppies had to be fried and passed around, and then the shrimp. All the frying had to be done over an open flame outdoors, and a thermometer was essential. The whole process was too messy and too smelly for the home kitchen.

As soon as the fish came out of the oil, it had to go directly onto a bed of absorbent paper towels. For serving trays, Chapman insisted on using the low-sided open boxes that cases of soda pop cans come in. These were set up in advance, and each one went inside a paper grocery sack, which served as an impromptu warming oven for the fried fish. It was an ingenious system. The first few batches of cooked fish went onto a cardboard tray and right into a waiting paper bag; the fish stayed perfectly warm while the subsequent batches were fried. As the third and fourth batches of fish were fried, the guests started on the buffet line, and as they were seated, the cardboard platters made their way around the table.

The day that we held the fish fry at my house, we set up a long table on the lawn. The restaurant had purchased a portable burner and rented chairs. It rained all morning, and I was afraid it would rain all day. But I started the baked beans and set up the portable burner. Canlis's general manager showed up early and he set out the chairs just as the rain let up. Chapman, with the help of my school-age boys, put together the hush puppy batter. By the time the rest of the crew arrived, the sun wasn't exactly shining, but the rain had stopped, and the garden shone in a warm, overcast glow. The beans came out of the oven, and the blackberry cobblers went in. Pitchers of iced tea and lemonade appeared. Bottles of beer and wine were opened, and the fried hush puppies made their rounds on plates lined with paper towels.

Sitting down to eat, some crew members held babies on their laps. Kids wandered freely in and around the line by the buffet table, and birds sang from the fig trees. I ran back and forth from the fry station by the garage to the table on the lawn, bouncing in and out of the kitchen for last-minute necessities. Then I took a plate and sat down.

I had only ten or fifteen minutes at the table, but there was during that time a kind of stillness that felt familiar. The plain Floridian food, the murmur of all those voices, and the warmth of the sun as it penetrated the thin veil of clouds came together in one beautiful moment, and I whispered to someone sitting beside me, "I love this." It was that moment, surrounded by all my coworkers and their families, that I had hoped for when I invited Chapman to do the fish fry. Even though I was thousands of miles away and in completely different circumstances, I felt that same easy, timeless kind of eternity that I sensed that day in the hospital when I went to see Alice Canlis's mother. I was home.

These days, a five-gallon fish fryer with a portable propane tank resides in my garage, and I am prepared, if the need arises, to do a big Pensacola-style fish fry like Chapman Creighton did that day. But I seldom do. Instead, I re-create a handful of those dishes in scaled-down proportions for a family supper. Each of the following recipes makes six servings, but so many dishes are served at a fish fry like this that if you made everything at once, there could be enough food to feed twice that many people.

My frying follows a scripted sequence. Hush puppies are first in a relatively cool 325°F fryer. Next come the shrimp (actually jumbo prawns), which are best fried at 350°F. And finally, thin fillets of snapper or pollock, which fry best at

375°F. Canned baked beans can be warmed in the oven while the rest of the meal is prepared. Serve the hush puppies and shrimp as appetizers; serve potato salad, coleslaw, and baked beans with the fish.

FLORIDA-STYLE POTATO SALAD

Florida potato salad is made with starchy baking potatoes, not the waxy potatoes that most cooks prefer, and the eggs for the salad are boiled right in the pot with the spuds. Another peculiarity of this recipe from Chapman Creighton involves boiling the onion and celery; it sounds bizarre, but it produces an amazingly mild and tender version of this classic American picnic staple.

> 2½ pounds (about 3 large) russet potatoes, whole and unpeeled
>
> 3 eggs
>
> ½ medium sweet onion, peeled and diced
>
> I stalk celery, diced
>
> 2 medium dill pickles, plus I tablespoon pickle juice
>
> ¾ cup mayonnaise
>
> 2 tablespoons yellow mustard
>
> Kosher salt and freshly ground black pepper

◇ Put the potatoes in a large pot and cover them with water. Cook over high heat until the water is boiling, then reduce the heat to low and cook for 15 minutes, or until the potatoes are barely fork tender. Nestle the eggs in among the simmering potatoes and cook for 10 minutes longer, or until the potatoes are tender and their skins have begun to split. Drain the potatoes and eggs in a colander. Spread the hot potatoes out on a baking sheet or a tray to cool, and put the eggs in a bowl of cold water.

◇ While the eggs and potatoes are cooling, prepare the dressing. In a small saucepan, bring 2 cups water to a boil. When the water is boiling, put the onion and celery into the saucepan and cook for 2 or 3 minutes, or until tender. Drain the onion and celery in a colander and transfer them to a large mixing bowl. Grate the pickles through the largest holes of a box-style cheese grater directly into the bowl with the celery and onion; stir in the mayonnaise and mustard and add the pickle juice to make a smooth dressing. Add salt and pepper to taste.

◇ Peel the eggs and rinse them in cold water. Grate the eggs through the largest holes of the box-style cheese grater into the dressing. Peel the potatoes; the skins should slip right off. Cut the potatoes into 1-inch chunks and add them to the dressing. Toss to coat. Taste for seasoning and add more salt and pepper if desired. Keep the potato salad refrigerated until serving time.

Makes 6 servings

COLESLAW

When I make Chapman's coleslaw, I have to force myself not to add onions, and I resist the urge to add a dash of sesame oil, a practice I picked up from the pantry cooks at Canlis. When I follow the simple directives of the old master, I rediscover the pure joy of plain coleslaw.

¼ cup white vinegar

1 ½ teaspoons pickling spice

¼ cup sugar

1 ½ teaspoons kosher salt

1 cup Homemade Mayonnaise (page 123)

1 small head green cabbage

¼ pound (about 2 large) carrots, peeled and grated

Freshly ground black pepper

◇ To make the dressing, cook the vinegar and pickling spice in a saucepan over high heat just until the mixture begins to boil. Turn off the heat, allow the spices to steep in the vinegar for 5 minutes, and then strain the liquid into a mixing bowl and whisk in the sugar and salt. Whisk in the mayonnaise and place the bowl in the refrigerator to chill.

◇ To finish the coleslaw, quarter the cabbage and pull away any wilted or damaged outer leaves. Cut out the tough cores from each quarter, then slice the cabbage quarters as thinly as you can; use a mandoline, or simply slice the cabbage with a sharp chef's knife. Pile the sliced cabbage and grated carrots into the chilled dressing and toss to coat. Add pepper to taste.

Makes about 1 quart, serving 6

HUSH PUPPIES

These savory corn bread fritters used to be made from leftover fish-frying batter. The fried batter was supposed to be tossed to the dogs to calm them down so that folks could enjoy their fish. In fact, I've never seen anyone give hush puppies to the dogs. They're too tasty to give up, and they make a perfect hors d'oeuvre for your guests while they wait for the fish to fry.

½ small onion, peeled and roughly chopped

1 jalapeño pepper, roughly chopped

¾ cup lager-style beer or pale ale

1 cup self-rising cornmeal

½ cup self-rising flour

½ teaspoon baking powder

½ teaspoon kosher salt

Corn or canola oil, for frying

◇ Put the onion and jalapeño pepper in a food processor and process until very finely chopped. Transfer the mixture to a large mixing bowl and stir in the beer. Set aside.

◇ Pour the cornmeal, flour, baking powder, and salt into a paper bag and shake. Add the cornmeal mixture all at once to the beer mixture and stir until the mixture comes together to form a fairly soft dough. Let the dough stand for at least 1 hour before frying it.

◇ To fry the hush puppies, heat the oil to 325°F. To make finger-size hush puppies in the style of Pappy Creighton, press some of the dough onto a spatula to make an even layer about ½-inch thick. With the back of a knife, cut the hush puppy dough off the spatula in ½-inch strips, sliding the strips into the oil as you go. Alternatively, simply scoop tablespoon-size dollops of the dough directly into the oil. Fry for 3 to 5 minutes, or until well crisped and cooked through. Drain on paper towels. Repeat with the remaining dough and serve at once.

Makes 36 small fritters, serving 6

FRIED SHRIMP

The extra-firm texture and slightly sweet flavor of wild Gulf prawns distinguish them from farm-raised tiger prawns. Harvested using nets with escape hatches to minimize bycatch, these white prawns were traditionally referred to as "shrimp" on the Gulf Coast, regardless of their size. Chapman Creighton insisted on the jumbo size, which come 16 to 20 per pound.

> 1 pound Gulf prawns (16 to 20 count)
> Corn or canola oil, for frying
> ¼ cup cornmeal
> ¼ cup flour
> Sea salt and freshly ground black pepper

◇ Peel the prawns and split them lengthwise along the backside to devein them. Rinse them under cold running water and keep them on ice until a few minutes before serving time.

◇ Just before frying, heat the oil in a deep, heavy pot or a deep fryer to 350°F. Line a baking sheet with several layers of paper towels. Put the cornmeal and flour in a brown paper bag and shake to combine. Working with 6 shrimp at a time, sprinkle them with salt and pepper and pile them into the grocery bag with the flour and cornmeal mixture. Shake to coat.

◇ Slip the floured prawns into the hot oil and fry for 3 minutes, or until they float to the surface. Lift them from the hot oil and transfer them to the baking sheet lined with paper towels. Repeat with the remaining prawns and serve at once.

Makes 6 servings

FRIED FISH

For his Florida fish fries, Chapman Creighton preferred red snapper. But snapper is overharvested now, almost to the point of being an endangered species. Sadly, many of them are unintentionally captured in shrimp nets that don't have proper escape hatches. Trawl-caught at mid-depths in the Bering Sea, where bycatch is almost nil, wild Alaska pollock is a good alternative. If the fish is purchased frozen, let it thaw slowly overnight in the refrigerator; a rushed thawing time can compromise the texture of the fish.

> 3 pounds (about 6 fillets) Alaska pollock or Pacific cod fillets
> Corn and canola oil, for frying
> 1 ½ cups cornmeal
> Sea salt and freshly ground black pepper

◇ Trim the fillets to remove the dark and thin bits near the tail. Cut out any remaining pin bones and divide each fillet into 2 pieces. Rinse each fillet and place it on a thick layer of ice. Fish may be prepared up to this point several hours or even a day in advance.

◇ Just before frying, heat the oil in a deep, heavy pot or a deep fryer to 375°F. Preheat the oven to 250°F and line a baking sheet with several layers of paper towels. Put the cornmeal in a brown paper bag. Working with 4 pieces of fish at a time, sprinkle the ice-cold fillets with salt and pepper and pile them into the grocery bag with the cornmeal. Shake to coat the fillets with cornmeal. Slip the cornmeal-covered fish fillets into the hot oil and fry for 4 minutes, or until the fish floats to the surface. Let the fish sizzle in the oil for another 30 seconds.

◇ Lift the fillets out of the hot oil and transfer them to the prepared baking sheet. Keep the fried fish in the warm oven while you prepare subsequent batches. Serve the first batch of fish as the last batch is being fried.

Makes 6 servings

MERROIR

*"Saltspray, rust, and a picklelike crunch. Then sweetness,
nori, and the lingering grassy richness of raw milk. I felt
an inner surge of Paleolithic zeal. This was the oyster
that had beckoned me across the continent."*

—ROWAN JACOBSEN

J ust as a glass of wine calls to mind the piece of earth from
which it sprang, an oyster brings to the table a drop of the
water in which it was raised. But unlike the nuanced *terroir* in
the wine bottle, which can be difficult to grasp, the "merroir"
in an oyster shell is quite easily detected.

Because so much depends on where and how an oyster
is raised, oysters are typically named for their home waters.
As Waverley Root pointed out in *Food: An Authoritative and
Visual History and Dictionary of the Foods of the World*: "Take
seedling oysters from the same bed in Brittany, plant them in
Whitstable, Belon, and Marennes, and you will harvest three
completely different types of oysters." This is because each
body of water has its own peculiar thumbprint of salinity and

dissolved minerals, and, more important, its own unique population of flora upon which the bivalves feed. The oysters will not only taste different, they'll look different, too; depending on how much time they spend underwater and how much time they spend above the tide line, their shells will have different thicknesses.

Standing beside the shell-shaped bowl of Totten Inlet at low tide on a winter evening, and mulling over that just-hatched notion of merroir, I couldn't help noticing that the clouds whirled above my head in the pattern of an oyster's markings. The receding tide lapped at the shore the same way an oyster's liquor splashes inside its shell, and the very air was filled with the fresh saltwater smell of mollusks. I had the sense that the world itself was an oyster—not *my* oyster, per se, but an oyster nonetheless.

The particular piece of beach on which I stood is home to a shellfish growing operation managed by Taylor Shellfish Farms, which runs more than half a dozen farms from Willapa Bay on the southern coast of Washington State to Samish Bay near the northern end. The Taylor family has been farming oysters in Washington for more than a century, and company president Bill Taylor was my host. My friend and Taylor company spokesperson Jon Rowley had called together a dozen oyster aficionados to brave the cold on a January night in 2003 to sample these delectable bivalves at the source. Oysters tend to be at their best in winter; winter tides in Washington are low in the middle of the night, and oysters must be harvested at low tide. So there we were in the cold, in the dark, and up to our ankles in oysters.

Oysters have been growing here with and without human intervention for considerably longer than the century or so that the Taylors and other oyster farmers have been coaxing them along, and their range is even greater than the considerable scope outlined by the holdings of Taylor Shellfish. Even before the first people wandered these shores thousands of years ago, oysters thrived from Baja, California, to Sitka, Alaska. Those first oysters were of one variety: the Olympia (*Ostrea lurida*). A diminutive oyster with colossal flavor, it was nearly harvested out of existence when entrepreneurs started shipping oysters to San Francisco in the wake of the California Gold Rush in the 1850s. By the turn of the century, a single Oly brought a silver dollar in the fancy dining salons where every diner was a Diamond Jim Brady wannabe.

As long as Washington remained a territory, oysters and the tidelands where they grew technically belonged to the Native Americans. But harvesting went on willy-nilly wherever the shellfish grew close enough to the open waters of the Pacific to make shipping them out a feasible enterprise. Over the decades following Washington's admission to the Union, changes in legislation allowed oyster growers to purchase and lease the oyster beds. By 1900, though, over-harvesting had rendered the once-abundant Northwest stocks thoroughly depleted. Dikes were built to extend the oyster beds, and restocking efforts kept the industry alive.

Attempts were made to establish Eastern oysters (*Crassostrea virginica*) as early as 1894, but in 1917, for reasons that remain unclear, all the stocks died out. Recent efforts to reintroduce Eastern oysters to Northwest waters have been more successful. Our little band of foragers agreed that the plump and juicy Virginicas we tasted that night on Totten Inlet were just about as good as any oysters we had ever tasted, and since then, a number of more authoritative voices in the industry have agreed. The late *New York Times* food writer R. W. Apple Jr. called them "uncommonly plump and sweet, with a memorably pronounced mineral finish."

Rowan Jacobsen, author of *A Geography of Oysters*, revisited oysters in his 2010 book, *American Terroir*, and noted that, at a tasting of twenty different Virginica oysters from various oyster farms around the country, the oysters from Totten Inlet were "the best of the best."

But on that night in January, we were equally thrilled with other varieties. We swooned over a few wonderfully metallic European flats (*Ostrea edulis*). These European natives are the species that made Belon, a town in Brittany whose name is synonymous with oysters, and for a while almost any European flat, regardless of where it was grown, was called a Belon. But that's like calling a sparkling wine from California champagne. We cherished the tiny Olympias and availed ourselves of the crinkly, deep-cupped Kumamotos (*Crassostrea sikamea*). We devoured dozens of Pacifics (*Crassostrea gigas*); fast growing and remarkably sweet, these oysters dominate the market, and for good reason.

Since that night, Rowley has organized what he calls "Walrus and Carpenter Picnics" for others who wish to experience the oyster beds at night. Named after the poem in Lewis Carroll's *Through the Looking Glass*, the picnics start when revelers board a bus on the Seattle waterfront at 6:30 at night. After a ferry ride across the Puget Sound, the curious shellfish aficionados arrive at the oyster beds, where wines are poured and oysters are shucked by a bonfire on the beach. Then, back on board the warm bus, the satiated adventurers are served oyster stew.

HOT SAUSAGES AND COLD OYSTERS

When I cooked for Martha Stewart at the home of a mutual friend, I served cold Virginica oysters and hot andouille sausages as passed hors d'oeuvres. When she ignored the rest of the guests for a few minutes and joined me in the kitchen, Martha impressed me with both her ability to shuck and her ability to slurp. The spicy, hot sausages with overtones of garlic afford the perfect snappy break between oysters, which, when served like this, need no sauce. I like to use Uli's Famous Cajun Andouilles from Pike Place Market, but any good spicy sausage will do.

If they have been properly handled, oysters need not be washed after you bring them home, but if they carry some detritus from the sea, don't hesitate to give them a quick rinse in cold water before shucking them. Do not, however, soak them in tap water or rinse them after they are shucked; they should retain a bit of the seawater in which they were grown.

> 1 tablespoon olive oil
> 1 pound andouille sausages
> Crushed ice, for serving
> 3 dozen medium-size fresh oysters, live in their shells

◇ Place one serving platter in the freezer and a second serving platter in a warm oven.

◇ Put the oil and sausages in a large heavy-bottomed skillet, preferably cast iron. Cook over medium-high heat, turning occasionally, until the sausages are sizzling and well browned, about 10 minutes.

◇ While the sausages are browning, line the chilled serving platter with crushed ice. To shuck each oyster, hold it securely with a dish towel in one hand, and insert the shucking knife about ⅛ inch at the "hinge," which is the more pointed end, where the whirls appear to come together. Give the knife a firm twist, turning to unhinge the top shell, and then slip the knife in farther (keeping the knife close to the top shell and away from the meat inside) to free the top shell entirely. After the shell is removed, shimmy the knife gently under the oyster flesh to loosen it from the bottom shell, which becomes its serving dish. As they are shucked, rest the oysters in shells on the bed of crushed ice.

◇ When the sausages are browned, lift them out of the pan and cut them into 1-inch lengths. Pile the cut sausages on the warm platter and poke each piece with a bamboo pick or a toothpick. Serve alongside the shucked oysters.

Makes 6 servings

OYSTER STEW OR BISQUE

The only real difference between an oyster stew and an oyster bisque is that the bisque is pureed while the stew is not. When I make oyster stew, I like to season it with a little ginger, but when I make oyster bisque, I leave out the ginger and add a splash of sherry instead. If I'm serving the dish as a main course, I leave the oysters whole and allow at least six per person. If the soup is the first course in a big dinner, then I puree it and serve a little less. I like this soup best when it's made with Virginicas, but Pacifics are also nice and are more widely available.

> 2 dozen medium oysters, live in their shells
> ¼ cup unsalted butter
> I large shallot, finely chopped
> ½-inch piece ginger root, grated on a Microplane grater or finely chopped (optional)
> ¼ cup dry sherry (optional)
> 2 cups heavy cream, preferably organic
> Freshly ground black pepper

◇ Scrub the oysters if they have anything clinging to them (most well-grown oysters are sprayed forcefully before they go to market, so this might not be necessary). Pile the oysters into a large kettle with 1 cup of water, and steam them over high heat until the shells are loosened and the oysters have begun to open, about 6 minutes. Take the oysters out of the pot and let them stand until they are cool enough to handle. Strain the steaming liquid through a paper towel–lined sieve and reserve it.

◇ Rinse the pot and melt the butter over medium heat. Sauté the shallot until it is soft and translucent, about 5 minutes. Add the ginger or sherry and the cream. Turn the heat up to high; bring the cream to a full, rolling boil; then pour in the reserved oyster steaming liquid. Reduce the heat to low. Take the steamed oysters out of their shells and warm them in the soup for a minute before serving. If the soup is to be a bisque, puree it with an immersion blender before distributing it among serving bowls.

Makes 4 entrée servings or 6 appetizer servings

BORSCHT

"The beet is the most intense of vegetables. The radish, admittedly,
is more feverish, but the fire of the radish is a cold fire, the
fire of discontent not of passion. Tomatoes are lusty enough, yet
there runs through tomatoes an undercurrent of frivolity.
Beets are deadly serious."

—TOM ROBBINS

The scent of earth is so pronounced in a beet that it rede-
fines the word "terroir." And yet, liberated of its earthy
aroma, the beet tastes not of minerals or soil, but of sugar,
pure and simple. Beets are fundamentally sweet, and that, I
suppose, is why those of us who love them have found a way
to get past the aura and into the heart of the thing. Plug your
nose and drink a glass of beet juice; it's pure sugar water.

But the real meaning of the thing, if you ask me, the raison
d'être for a beet, is borscht. Anyone who learns to love beets
comes, sooner or later, to love borscht. The very name evokes
an older world, a simpler time when people ate food grown in
the ground on which they walked. It's almost hard not to picture the peasant farmer pulling beets from the ground, shaking
off the dirt, and putting them on to boil.

Borscht can be as simple as a cold beet puree finished with sour cream. But more often than not, it's a lavish combination of beets and meats like the "Borscht on a Grand Scale" described in the *Soups* volume of Time Life's 1979 The Good Cook series. The editors of that series devoted several pages just to cooking the meats—a beef shank, a chuck roast, a ham hock, and a rasher of lean salt pork. But that's the easy part.

"The first step in making this or any borscht," say the editors, "takes place several days in advance of actual cooking." Apparently, the most authentic versions of borscht in Russia, Poland, and the Ukraine call for "beet liquor"—a mixture of beets, rye bread, and water left to ferment for days to form a vinegary liquid that gives the soup its distinctive tangy edge. Without that beet liquor, it would seem, beet soup just isn't borscht. It's no wonder that so many of the people who read The Good Cook series decided that real, authentic cooking was just too intense and opted instead to open a can of soup and read about making the real thing.

Other sources present equally intimidating methods. My 1961 edition of *Larousse Gastronomique*, with a preface by Escoffier himself, includes four distinct versions of the soup. One of them demands that we "add a small duck browned in the oven, a pound of blanched brisket of beef, and a rasher of bacon" to make the soup worthy of our efforts. So much for the old master's dictum to "keep it simple."

But if the old versions are too complex, newer formulas for borscht seem almost too simple. The *Joy of Cooking* offers a recipe in which canned tomatoes predominate. The 2005 edition of *The Gourmet Cookbook* advises us to start with a jar of pickled beets. *The Best Recipe: Soups and Stews* by the editors of *Cook's Illustrated* aims for streamlined authenticity, but tedious explanations of every step exhaust me before I even make it to the kitchen.

I like to imagine that if I had a grand old farm in the Old World style, I could produce everything I need to make a borscht any Russian peasant would be proud of. I'd start with beets, carrots, potatoes, cabbage, and onions right out of the garden. The beef and the broth would come from my own steer, and the sour cream would be lifted off this morning's milk, drawn from my own cow.

Alas, I live in the New World, and my "farm" is a modest acre on Bainbridge Island. The only element for borscht you'll find in my garden is the potatoes. Still, I get stunning beets from the local farmers market, and cabbage and carrots, too. I don't have my own steer, and I never seem to have an extra duck, but I do keep the freezer stocked with grass-fed beef. In lieu of that elusive fermented beet liquor, I always have balsamic vinegar on hand; and to go with the vinegar, I have olive oil to make up for the fatty salt pork. With a little imagination, a good store-bought organic sour cream or yogurt tastes almost homemade, and before you know it, my borscht seems downright bona fide.

NEW AMERICAN BORSCHT

Tailored to match the tastes and sensibilities of twenty-first-century cooks, this version of the traditional Eastern European soup might not be perfectly authentic, but, made with the freshest local and natural ingredients, it does provide a certain sense of place.

For the beets

2 large beets, unpeeled, with tails intact

For the soup base

1 ½ pounds stewing beef - *organic*
1 tablespoon kosher salt
2 tablespoons sugar
2 tablespoons balsamic vinegar
2 quarts beef broth - *organic*
1 bay leaf

For the vegetable sauté

2 tablespoons olive oil
1 medium onion, peeled and cut into small dice
2 medium carrots, peeled and cut into small dice
3 or 4 small yellow-fleshed potatoes, unpeeled, cut into medium dice
½ head Napa cabbage

For finishing the soup

Kosher salt and freshly ground black pepper
Chopped parsley or dill, for garnish
1 cup plain yogurt or sour cream (optional)

◇ To prepare the beets, place them in a saucepan with 4 cups water. Over high heat, bring the water to a full, rolling boil. Reduce the heat to low and simmer the beets until they are tender, about 1 hour.

◇ While the beets are cooking, prepare the soup base. Sprinkle the beef with the salt. Stir the sugar in a dry heavy-bottomed Dutch oven or soup kettle over medium-high heat until the sugar melts and begins to turn brown, about 5 minutes; when the sugar is a deep caramel color, add the beef. Stir the beef around until it is well browned, about 2 minutes, then add the balsamic vinegar, beef broth, and bay leaf. Bring the liquid to a boil, reduce the heat to low, cover, and simmer the beef until it is tender, about 1 hour.

◇ While the beets and beef are still cooking, prepare the vegetable sauté. Warm the olive oil in a large frying pan over medium-high heat, add the onion and carrots, and sauté until they are beginning to brown, about 5 minutes. Add the potatoes and cabbage and sauté just until the vegetables are heated through. Add the sautéed vegetables to the beef base and continue simmering until the potatoes are tender, about 15 minutes.

◇ Use a slotted spoon to lift the beets out of the boiling water and, under cold running water, slip off their skins. Cut the cooked, peeled beets into batons, about 2 inches long and ½ inch wide; add the cut beets to the soup. Season the soup to taste with salt and pepper, ladle it into serving bowls, and garnish with a pinch of chopped parsley or dill. Pass yogurt or sour cream separately.

Makes 8 servings

PUMPERNICKEL BREAD

If making truly authentic borscht is intimidating, so is making its traditional accompaniment, the dark rye bread known as pumpernickel. I have always inclined toward the not-overly-delayed-gratification school of cooking that allows me to produce something reasonably good in a reasonable amount of time. Armed with a formula from the 1969 edition of Homemade Bread *by the food editors of* Farm Journal *for a jumping off point, I developed a formula in the early seventies for pumpernickel that serves me well to this day. Leftover mashed potatoes are essential here, so if you don't have any on hand, quickly cook and mash a potato and cool it to room temperature while the dough is getting underway.*

1 cup warm water (85°F to 95°F)

1 tablespoon active dry yeast

2 cups bread flour, divided

1 cup mashed potatoes, at room temperature

¼ cup molasses

¼ cup cocoa powder

1 tablespoon kosher salt

2 cups rye flour

◇ In the bowl of an electric mixer or in a large mixing bowl, stir together the water, yeast, and 1 cup of the bread flour. Allow the mixture to stand until it is actively bubbling and has risen to twice its initial volume, about 30 minutes.

◇ Use the paddle attachment or a strong wooden spoon to slowly stir the remaining bread flour, mashed potatoes, molasses, cocoa powder, and salt into the yeast mixture until a thick, sticky batter is formed. Mix in 1 cup of the rye flour.

◇ Switch to the dough hook or turn the dough out onto a floured work surface. Knead in enough of the remaining 1 cup of rye flour to create a fairly stiff dough that springs back when pressed.

◇ Return the dough to the bowl and cover it with a damp, lint-free kitchen towel or with a piece of plastic wrap. Let it rise in a warm place until doubled in size, about 1 hour.

◇ Heavily dust a baking sheet with rye flour. Press the risen dough down in the bowl to punch out the air, turn it out onto a lightly floured surface, and roll it into a rectangle about 10 inches wide by 12 inches long. Starting at one of the short ends, roll the dough like a jelly roll, pressing it firmly to form a log. Place the loaf on the prepared baking sheet and let it rise until almost doubled in size, about 30 minutes. While the loaf is rising, preheat the oven to 375°F.

◇ Bake the risen loaf until it is browned on top and sounds hollow when tapped, about 40 minutes; an instant-read thermometer inserted in the center of the loaf will register about 195°F. Transfer the loaf from the baking sheet onto a cooling rack and cool to room temperature before slicing.

Makes 1 large loaf

GROWING FARMERS

"Agriculture is our wisest pursuit, because it will in the end contribute most to real wealth, good morals, and happiness."
—THOMAS JEFFERSON

We had been driving for an hour and a half, and the sun was still barely cresting the horizon. I was with my friend Jon Rowley, who is, as far as I can tell, on a lifelong quest for the best-tasting foods in the world. His business card has no job title because, he says, that allows him to do whatever he wants, but others have called him all sorts of exonerative things. When they listed him in their annual roundup of their hundred favorite people, places, and things in 2008, the editors of *Saveur* magazine gave him the title "Disciple of Flavor." Basically, he's a consultant who hooks up producers with folks who can sell their products, and he is ever on the prowl for new and interesting things to promote. From time to time, he invites me to join him on one of his culinary adventures.

This particular adventure was originally planned as a carrot crusade, and our destination was to be the home of one Nash Huber, carrot farmer. Nash's carrots are somewhat famous in Seattle because, among the peculiar set of folks who pay attention to things like this, his carrots are considered the sweetest carrots grown in the state.

A farmer who cultivates some 400 acres of land on various small plots near Sequim, Washington, Nash Huber grew up on a 180-acre Illinois farm and came to Washington in 1979, when he was in his thirties, armed with a degree in chemistry. But when he came to the Dungeness Valley, he saw an opportunity to apply his understanding of soil chemistry to growing organic vegetables in what he perceived was some of the best soil in North America. Today, his small plots provide produce and grain for eleven neighborhood farmers markets and nine PCC Natural supermarkets around Puget Sound.

Unfortunately, by the time Rowley and I found a mutually agreed-upon date to visit Huber, all the carrots had been harvested for the season. We instead found ourselves catching the tail end of parsnip season.

"I don't seem to have those directions," said Rowley. "I must have left them on my desk. See if you can use my phone to call and get directions." I tried, but out there on the peninsula, cell phone reception can be sketchy.

"Let's just ask someone," I said. A few blocks down the road we saw an elderly woman in a yellow coat. "Excuse me," I said. "Do you happen to know a fellow named Nash Huber?"

"I don't think so," she said, eyeing me suspiciously. She looked past me into the cab at Jon.

"He's a farmer," said Jon. "Grows carrots."

"Oh," she said, "you mean that organic fellow. Sure, I know Nash Huber. Grows carrots. You take your next left. His place is the second house on the left, lots of trees. Are you boys headed to the men's breakfast?"

"We are."

"Well, he lives right over there. You'll see a few cars out front. The place with all the trees."

"Thank you," we said.

I had imagined that we were going directly to a farm. But as it turned out, Huber's house is in a suburban neighborhood. Inside, pressed between wall-to-wall bookshelves and a baby grand piano, was a table surrounded by an odd assortment of chairs, each inhabited by a man with a plate. More men were in the kitchen pulling waffles out of a waffle iron, pouring coffee, and putting the final touches on a pan full of something they called "parsnip fritter." Huber was hosting one of his weekly men's breakfasts.

Every Thursday since 1992, a group of a dozen or so men have gathered to share food they have grown or prepared with their own hands. It may seem odd that while most twenty-first-century social gatherings seem to be organized by or at least fully inclusive of women, this group spontaneously formed around the friendship among men. The gathering did not attract the women in their lives, with one exception—wives and girlfriends join the men every Thanksgiving.

"This whole breakfast thing started about twenty years ago," says Huber, "when a few of us would gather at a local restaurant before our Thursday morning bike ride. It didn't take us too long to realize that we could probably make a better breakfast at home, and we knew we could make better coffee." So every Thursday morning, in anticipation of his friends' arrival, Huber starts the coffee.

Once the coffee is going, someone heads to the back room to bring out an extra table. Early arrivers set the table and Paul Hansen starts heating up the waffle iron. Hansen raises lamb for a living, but on Thursday mornings, he makes waffles from wheat grown on Huber's farms; it's ground to order every Wednesday. Mark Spencer, who works as a professional massage therapist every other day of the week, scrambles eggs. They might come from Huber's own farms, or from laying hens kept by several other members of the group. The oldest men in the group have been friends of Nash for decades. The youngest men at the table, now employed by Huber to work on his farms, might still have been in diapers when the men's breakfasts got started.

"When I came here in 1968, that boy's grandfather was the first man I met," said Huber with a tilt of his head toward Josh Gloor. Gloor now maintains the orchards, drives heavy equipment, and plants and harvests on the various farms Huber keeps throughout the valley.

"Most young men coming out of our community don't know who they are or what they are capable of," said Huber when we set off after breakfast for a tour of the largest of Huber's farms, the seventy-six-acre Delta Farm. "They're stuck inside watching TV. These young men are the main reason I do this farming. Farming, you see, gives young people an identity."

"In 1959," said Huber, "the general budget for this county was somewhere in the neighborhood of $500,000. The population was about 33,000. Fifteen percent of that budget was spent on criminal justice. Last year, the budget was $24 million and the percentage spent on criminal justice was closer to 65 percent. But the population has only doubled!"

These baffling numbers gradually took on meaning as Nash continued. "We've changed our economy," he explained. "We were once a stable, resource extracting economy. Now we're something else. Fishing and logging interests are gone." With land prices and taxes rising, most of the farms are gone, too, having given way to housing. "With more people and fewer farms, there's a shortage of jobs, so idle kids are getting into trouble. At the same time, the machinery set up to process petty crimes has become the county's biggest employer."

Before I had time to process these thoughts, we had arrived. I stepped out of the truck and surveyed the freshly dug, deep brown soil where carrots had recently been harvested. Frosted rows of cabbage and kale lay beyond. Delta Farm boasts a pigpen and a chicken coop, but it is primarily dedicated to row crops. Built on land purchased by the PCC Farmland Trust in 1999, it's been leased by Nash ever since. PCC, or Puget Consumers' Co-op, is a Seattle-based chain of natural foods stores, and its Farmland Fund is an independent, self-supporting, nonprofit land trust. The fund was established to ensure a steady supply of organic produce for the stores, but founders knew it would also help check the conversion of agricultural land into residential areas. Delta Farm in Dungeness was the foundation's first purchase.

"This used to be a dairy farm," said Huber. "And the local milk was prized because it had a higher cream content than just about any other milk in the state." Butterfat content is what ultimately determines the market value of milk. "Cows, you see, transform the energy contained in the grass into energy in the form of butterfat. If the grass is richer in sugar, the milk is richer in cream." What makes the grass in this valley richer is a confluence of melting glacial water from the nearby Olympic Mountains that infuses the soil with a high mineral content, and a relatively high proportion of sunny days brought on by the rain shadow of the Olympics themselves.

The same high ratio of sunny days now prompts thousands of retirees to move into the valley, expanding pavement and covering farmland as they come. But the farmland that does remain has the same rich soil. "The factors that once contributed to making grazing land particularly good for cattle now make for incredibly sweet root vegetables," said Huber. "The minerals in the soil give the plants the strength to capture all that sunlight in the form of concentrated sugars. Why don't you gather up some of these parsnips that didn't get picked up when they harvested this field?" So Jon and I set about gathering as many parsnips as we could carry.

Later that day, I stopped by the farm stand where a couple of young farmers-in-training were selling the produce they had planted, grown, and harvested on Huber's farms. Together, Huber and his wife, Patty, who handles much of the farm management, employ about twenty-five people full time and more than twice that during peak growing season. Most of these folks are still in their twenties, but a handful of those have stayed on for more than eight years, and they see working for the Hubers as an opportunity to learn a meaningful trade that will support them for the rest of their lives.

"When they first start out, we can only pay the interns a little above minimum wage," says Patty. But working on the farm has certain benefits. "Some of them camp out all summer on the farm, and they all eat off the farm for free." For someone with a sense of adventure, it's a better life than working in a fast-food restaurant, which is the most common first job for young people in this country.

One of the operation's greatest success stories is a young woman named Kia Armstrong. "She was living in her car," says Patty, "and she needed a place to work, so we gave her a job. She's been with us seven or eight years. Now she's married and she owns a home in Sequim." Kia coordinates interns on the farm and schedules workers in the fields and at the eleven farmers markets where the produce is sold.

At the farm store, I bought some of the carrots that remained from the harvest we had just missed. I bought beets, winter squash, potatoes, and kale, and when I brought them home, the vegetables seemed to emanate the warmth and energy of the valley in which they were grown. But when I cooked and ate them, what I thought about was how producing and selling these vegetables had impacted the lives of the people who planted them, tended them, and brought them to the small farm store to sell.

It occurred to me that Nash and Patty Huber are raising more than livestock, vegetables, and grains; they are raising the next generation of farmers. At their Thursday breakfasts and in their fields, the Hubers are the glue that holds their community together. Watching Nash offer an encouraging word to a cancer survivor here or a proud dad there, I'd found that his interactions precisely parallel the way he adds minerals and organic matter to the soil. His words and his questions are placed thoughtfully and intentionally, with a little humor and a little wisdom, adding precisely what's needed to nurture what's growing, whether it's a field of carrots or an entire community.

HONEST WAFFLES

Unlike the guys who regularly make waffles at Nash Huber's men's breakfasts, I don't grind my own flour . . . yet. But I do like a good waffle now and then. My favorite waffles are made with buckwheat flour; since it has virtually no gluten, the waffles come out light and crisp. If I'm out of buckwheat flour, whole-wheat flour is a good second choice, especially if I can get my hands on some of the flour grown on Huber's farms. Good waffles can be whipped up from scratch in about 15 minutes. I tuck any extras into sandwich bags and freeze them. On weekdays, I can pop the frozen waffles in the toaster for a quick breakfast. If time is at a premium, I skip the butter and syrup and eat them out of hand, like toast.

> 1 cup unbleached all-purpose flour
> 1 cup buckwheat or whole-wheat flour
> 1 tablespoon baking powder
> 1 teaspoon kosher salt
> 2 eggs
> ¼ cup sugar
> ¼ cup corn oil or canola oil
> 1 ½ cups milk
> Maple syrup (optional)

◇ Preheat a waffle iron. In a small mixing bowl, whisk together the all-purpose flour, buckwheat flour, baking powder, and salt.

◇ In a medium mixing bowl, whisk the eggs with the sugar and, still whisking, stream in the oil. Whisk in the milk, then add the flour mixture all at once, stirring just enough to bring the ingredients together. Do not overmix or the waffles will be tough.

◇ If the waffle iron is not well seasoned, rub a little butter over the surface or spray it with nonstick spray. Spoon the batter (about ½ cup per waffle) onto the hot iron and close it. Steam will come pouring out for about 3 minutes, then it will slow down and cease altogether. When the steam slows down, peek at the waffles, and when they are golden brown, after about 5 minutes, remove them from the iron and serve hot with maple syrup.

Makes 4 large waffles

SAGE-SCENTED BREAKFAST SAUSAGES

Ever since I started buying pork a half pig at a time, it has become more precious to me. For one thing, pastured natural pork is more expensive than the factory farmed commodity stuff. But I cherish it especially because the pork seems more connected to a living animal. When I open one of the one-pound packs of ground pork, I want to make it into something special. We still occasionally buy sausage from the store, but homemade is much better. These sausages are ostensibly for breakfast, but with a batch of parsnip fritters and some sautéed greens, they also make a fine supper.

1 pound ground pork, preferably all-natural, pastured pork
1 tablespoon sugar
1 tablespoon kosher salt
2 teaspoons ground sage
1 teaspoon freshly ground black pepper
½ teaspoon dried red chile flakes
¼ cup water
2 tablespoons lard or corn oil

◇ In a small mixing bowl, combine the pork, sugar, salt, sage, pepper, and chile flakes. This can be accomplished with a wooden spoon, but it's easier with cold, wet hands. Rinse your hands in cold tap water and go for it. If the mixture gets too sticky, rinse your hands again. Divide the mixture into 8 pieces and press each piece into a disk about 3 inches across; the sausage patties will cook best if they are slightly thinner in the middle than they are around the edges.

◇ Heat the water with the lard or the corn oil in a sauté pan over medium heat and add the sausages. Cook until the water has evaporated and the sausages have begun to brown in the remaining oil. Turn the sausages over and continue cooking until they are well browned and heated through, about 12 minutes in all.

Makes 4 generous servings

PARSNIP FRITTERS

Some older recipes for parsnip fritters call for the roots to be boiled, mashed, and then mixed with eggs and flour. I have better results when I mix raw, grated parsnips with the other ingredients and fry them in butter or oil.

1 egg
1 pound parsnips, peeled
¼ cup flour
½ teaspoon baking powder
1 teaspoon kosher salt
½ teaspoon freshly ground black pepper
2 tablespoons unsalted butter, divided into 6 pieces

◇ Preheat a griddle or a large cast-iron skillet over medium-high heat.

◇ Crack the egg into a small mixing bowl and beat it lightly with a fork. Grate the parsnips directly into the bowl and stir to combine with the egg.

◇ In a separate bowl, whisk together the flour, baking powder, salt, and pepper. Gently stir the dry ingredients into the parsnip mixture.

◇ Put the butter pieces on the griddle and scoop ⅓ cup of batter on top of each butter pat. Flatten the batter slightly to form 4-inch cakes. Allow the fritters to sizzle gently in the butter until they are well browned and crisp on the underside, about 5 minutes. Turn the fritters and cook for 3 minutes more, or until they are browned and cooked through.

Makes six 4-inch cakes

BON APPÉTIT!

"We need writers who persuade us that cooking is fun and that there is a wonderful creative satisfaction in going home and making a good meal at the end of the day."

—JUDITH JONES

When my wife and I took our boys to the Smithsonian National Museum of American History, the guys were fifteen and eleven. Our younger son, whose current passion was the history of weaponry, was determined to see a special exhibit: "The Price of Freedom: Americans at War." Our older son was less interested in weapons and more willing to see whatever came along. So while my wife accompanied the younger one to the war thing, I dragged our older son to see Julia Child's kitchen.

In 2001, at age eighty-nine, Julia left the home in Cambridge, Massachusetts, that she had lived in for forty-two years to return to her native California. Upon her departure, she graciously agreed to donate the kitchen with virtually everything in it to the Smithsonian's National Museum of American History. And now the fourteen-by-twenty-foot room that had been the scene of her popular cooking show is on display where anyone can go and see it. The blue-and-green-painted cabinets, the Marimekko print tablecloth covered in plastic, the oven that could accommodate two twenty-five pound turkeys, and about twelve hundred other items are all carefully preserved for posterity.

I never visited Julia in her kitchen, but I did meet her on several occasions, and she was consistently engaging, as witty and compelling in person as she was on television. Once, when I boarded an elevator on my way to the lobby of a hotel in New Orleans, Julia was already on board. I introduced myself, telling her that I was a chef working near Seattle, and that her work had inspired me when I was learning to cook. My mother, like virtually every other woman of her generation that I knew, had *Mastering the Art of French Cooking* on her cookbook shelf.

"Where did you study?" Julia wanted to know.

"I didn't go to culinary school," I said. "I'm self-taught."

"Never say you're self-taught, dear," she instructed me. "Always say you learned on the job." And then our elevator ride was over. But whenever I saw her after that, she remembered our brief conversation and asked me how things were in Seattle.

For millions of Americans, Julia may have been "the French Chef," but to me, she was all-American. Over the decades, she worked with and influenced American cooks from lots of different backgrounds and culinary traditions, and her life and work came to stand for what it means to cook and eat like an American, with all the inherent paradox that implies.

Ask any two Americans what American food is all about, and you'll likely get three or more answers. At 230-plus years of age, our young nation is still not very deeply rooted in its own culinary traditions. We borrow freely from other cultures even as we dismiss their cuisines as backward or too fussy. We will occasionally abandon foods we love at a word of advice from health authorities even as we cling to foods that we know are "bad" for us. We seem to be as confused about what to eat and what not to eat as any people have ever been. Michael Pollan calls it "our national eating disorder." Citing the Atkins craze as an example of "the American Paradox," Pollan paints us as "a notably unhealthy people obsessed by the idea of eating healthily." But Julia pooh-poohed the health-obsessed eaters and kept her fans on an even keel.

"I'd rather have a tiny bit of something really delicious," she once said, "than great gobs of something I don't like."

Like a lot of other American cooks, I was in awe of Julia's power to influence the way we ate, and occasionally disappointed in her refusal to endorse sustainably raised meats or organically grown vegetables. She was as quick to enjoy a hamburger as she was her own carefully wrought boeuf bourguignonne, and in neither case did she seem particularly interested in the provenance of the meat. When she first visited Alice Waters' Berkeley restaurant, Chez Panisse, where the menu cited sources for virtually every item, she seemed annoyed. "That's shopping," she said dismissively, "not cooking."

But her attitude was understandable in light of the generation from which she hailed. Born in 1912, she was younger than my grandmother, but older than my mother. Hers was a generation of Americans who saw bread lines and widespread hunger, as well as the rise of an industrialized food system that largely put an end to all that. And if Julia was never terribly fussy about how or where animals or plants were grown, she was exacting—even demanding—about how they were handled once those ingredients came into the kitchen.

Laura Shapiro's wise and funny book *Something from the Oven* describes how, in the wake of World War II, American food companies sought to find ways to keep assembly lines moving at the factories that had supplied rations for troops. The strategy was all about persuading the home cook to embrace ready-made and instant food products. Shapiro also authored one of the best and most insightful biographies of Child, in which she noted, "Determination was what mattered [to Julia], skill was the only shortcut [cooks] would ever need, and anything taking a long time was probably worth it. The food industry was spending millions to hammer home precisely the opposite message, but Julia had a source of power greater even than a national ad budget could purchase: people trusted her."

Every year, cookbook authors and food professionals gather at a conference hosted by an organization that Julia helped establish, the International Association of Culinary Professionals (IACP), to examine trends and traditions in food. The conference culminates in an award ceremony. The spring that I took my family to the Smithsonian, the conference was held in Seattle. The IACP Cookbook Award for best book in the American category went to Joan Nathan for her book *The New American Cooking*, which promised readers "new flavors from around the world."

When I heard of Nathan's win, I wondered if she described our food as a salmagundi of flavors from other places, as so many other authors on American food tend to do, or if she had some definitive way of determining what distinguishes it from other cuisines. As it turned out, Nathan's book provides both. There are fresh ways with old favorites like "Couscous from Timbuktu" and "Chicken Yasa from Gambia," as well as American originals like "Pancakes with Blue Corn" and "Nouvelle American Crabcakes." What is a home cook or an American diner to make of all this variety? And how do we choose what to eat?

I don't think there is any single, perfect definition for what constitutes American food, but I do think there is something essentially American about our approach to any task. Once we decide to take something seriously, the way we decided to take cooking seriously, we give it everything we've got. When Shapiro summarized what Julia Child taught us about cooking, she described what has essentially become the American attitude toward cooking:

> At the heart of every one of her television programs was a lesson—sometimes spoken outright and sometimes simply clear from the way she worked—about how to approach any task in the kitchen. It didn't matter whether you were planning to boil an egg or to spend the next two days making a galantine of turkey, the lesson was the same, and it was a moral template for American cooks. Use all your senses all the time, Julia instructed. Take pains with the work; do it carefully. Relish the details. Enjoy your hunger. And remember why you're there.

Fresh from my visit to the Smithsonian, and with Shapiro's words ringing in my head, I thought about all the different things Julia must have cooked in that iconic kitchen of hers. My mind wandered back there, and I remembered seeing a refrigerator magnet from Seattle's Pike Place Market, a place Julia truly loved, a place where I once heard her speak at a conference about the emerging Northwest food scene.

I thought that perhaps if she were still with us, I would like to walk with her through the stalls of that market and talk about American food. While we talked, we could gather ingredients for a simple lunch or dinner. I think I would make something uncomplicated and familiar, like a variation on the Bifteck Haché à la Lyonnaise, essentially a hamburger steak. For a side dish, I would make a contemporary version of succotash, a very American dish that Julia liked a lot. And for dessert, if it were summer, I would make that most American of desserts: strawberry shortcake, filled with tender Northwest-grown strawberries and rich organic whipped cream.

BIFTECK HACHÉ (HAMBURGER STEAK)

My family teases me when I make this dish, but when you buy a grass-fed steer a quarter animal at a time, you end up with a lot of ground beef in the freezer. Regular hamburgers are all well and good, but sometimes it's nice to allow the ground beef to stand on its own, albeit enhanced with a very Continental tasting sauce. Julia's Bifteck Haché à la Lyonnaise was fragrant with thyme and Worcestershire sauce, but her technique was unnecessarily complicated, I think. This streamlined version pays hom- age to the same set of flavors but comes together without as much fuss. If you're using a beef that's not so lean, you won't need as much olive oil for the initial browning of the steaks, but don't skimp on the butter; in the end, that red wine and butter sauce is what this dish is all about.

Red vermouth is the perfect red wine to keep on hand for dishes like this because even after it's opened, it keeps well for weeks in the pantry; ordinary wine grows sour-tasting and takes on off-putting smells quickly. Red vermouth is also great to have on hand for the occasional Manhattan cocktail, a perfect aperitif before a Bifteck Haché dinner.

1 ½ pounds lean ground grass-fed beef
1 tablespoon kosher salt
1 teaspoon freshly ground black pepper
4 tablespoons olive oil
2 large shallots, peeled and thinly sliced
⅓ cup red vermouth
3 tablespoons Worcestershire sauce
6 tablespoons unsalted butter, preferably organic

◇ With minimal handling, form the ground beef into 6 oval-shaped patties, each one about 4 inches across; sprinkle each one liber- ally with salt and pepper. Heat the olive oil in a large skillet over medium-high heat and transfer the patties to the hot pan.

◇ Sear the patties on one side until they are well browned (do not disturb them), about 2 minutes. Gently turn them over, taking care not to break them up, and sauté for about 2 minutes more, so that both sides are well browned. Transfer the patties to a baking sheet or a platter and cover with foil to keep them warm.

◇ Sauté the shallots in the fat left in the pan, stirring them and scraping up any browned bits of beef with a spatula, until the shallots are soft, about 1 minute. Stir in the vermouth and Worcestershire sauce and simmer, stirring, until the liquid is reduced to about a third of its original volume. Reduce the heat to medium-low and whisk in the butter to make a smooth sauce. Whisk in any juices from the patties that have accumulated on the baking sheet. Distribute the sauce over the hamburger steaks and serve at once.

Makes 6 servings

SUCCOTASH

Derived from a Narragansett Indian word, "succotash" is a dish of beans and corn that the first Americans taught the European settlers to make in the early 1600s. I like this version in which the more typical limas are replaced with green beans and tiny sweet tomatoes. Succotash is substantial enough to make a meal in itself, but it also makes an excellent side dish for grilled wild salmon or a grass-finished steak.

1 pound (about 4 cups) small green beans, trimmed

¾ pound (about 2 cups) corn kernels, cut off the cob

½ pound (about 1 generous cup) "Sweet 100" or grape tomatoes

¼ cup water

¼ cup (½ stick) unsalted butter

2 tablespoons sugar, preferably organic evaporated cane juice

1 tablespoon kosher salt

1 teaspoon white pepper

4 or 5 basil leaves, stemmed and cut into thin ribbons

◇ When the green beans, corn, and tomatoes are ready for cooking, place them near the stove. Put the water and butter in a large sauté pan over medium-high heat, and stir in the sugar, salt, and white pepper. When the butter is melted and the sugar and salt are dissolved, add the green beans and corn.

◇ Cook until the water evaporates and the vegetables have begun to sizzle in the butter, about 6 minutes. Add the tomatoes and cook, tossing or stirring gently with a wooden or silicone spatula just until the tomatoes are heated through, about 3 minutes longer.

◇ Just before serving, toss in the basil. Serve hot.

Makes 6 servings

STRAWBERRY SHORTCAKES

Julia never expressed much concern about where foods came from or how they were grown, but she did insist on using the freshest ingredients she could find. Fresh, ripe, and local are especially important qualities for strawberries because varieties that are grown to ship lack the tender, succulent qualities of the berries that are destined for local markets. I'm willing to forgo strawberries whenever they are out of season to wait for the best local ones to become available. Layered with warm, biscuit-like shortcakes and freshly whipped organic cream, they make one of America's all-time best desserts.

For the shortcakes

> 2 cups unbleached all-purpose flour
>
> 2 tablespoons sugar
>
> 1 tablespoon baking powder
>
> ½ teaspoon kosher salt
>
> ½ cup (1 stick) cold unsalted butter, preferably organic, cut into bits
>
> ¾ cup milk

For the berries

> 1 tablespoon freshly squeezed lemon juice
>
> ¼ cup sugar
>
> 2 pints ripe strawberries, preferably local and organic

For the topping

> 1 cup heavy cream, preferably organic
>
> ¼ cup powdered sugar
>
> ½ teaspoon vanilla extract
>
> Mint sprigs, for garnish

◇ Preheat the oven to 400°F and line a baking sheet with parchment paper.

◇ To make the shortcakes, in a food processor, combine flour, sugar, baking powder, and salt. Add the butter and pulse the motor on and off until the mixture is uniformly crumbly. Add the milk all at once and stir or process briefly to form a soft dough.

◇ Turn the dough out onto a well-floured surface and knead very lightly; do not overwork the dough, or the shortcakes will be tough. Roll the dough out to at least ½-inch thick, and with a biscuit cutter, cut 4-inch circles. Arrange the shortcakes a few inches apart on the prepared baking sheet and bake until the tops are lightly browned, 10 to 12 minutes.

◇ While the shortcakes are baking, prepare the strawberries. Put the lemon juice and sugar in a mixing bowl. Using a sharp paring knife, trim the crown off of each berry, removing as little fruit as possible. Cut the strawberries in half lengthwise, allowing the berries to fall into the bowl as they are cut. Toss the berries with the lemon juice and sugar to lightly coat and allow them to stand in the syrup.

◇ Whip the cream with the powdered sugar and vanilla extract. Pile the whipped cream into a ziplock food storage bag, then snip off one corner to create an impromptu piping bag.

◇ When the shortcakes are baked, cut each one in half. Put the bottom half of each shortcake on individual serving dishes. Distribute the strawberries evenly among the shortcakes, piling them directly onto the warm shortcake-halves. Pipe on the whipped cream. Plant the tops of the cakes over the whipped cream at a jaunty angle; tuck a mint sprig into each shortcake where the cake and berries meet, and serve at once.

Makes 6 servings

STILL LIFE WITH MAYONNAISE

"When she picked up her lunch the bag felt very light. She reached inside and there was only crumpled paper. They had taken her tomato sandwich."

—LOUISE FITZHUGH, FROM *HARRIET THE SPY*

Since I am both a chef and a writer, I am sometimes compelled to contemplate what cooking and writing have in common. What draws me to both pursuits is the simple joy I find in making something, and I have often said that baking a cake or writing a story satisfies the same impulse. I believe that this creative impulse is a basic human need. We all like to make things. And since I am not particularly good with power tools, I don't make houses.

But among creative outlets, cooking and writing are unique in that both endeavors produce something that ultimately becomes a part of whoever partakes in them. If I cook a meal and someone eats it, and if everything proceeds as it should, then something in that food will become a part of that person. If I read something and internalize that dialogue, then the words on the page will be incorporated into my own thoughts. Ideas expressed on the page will be reformulated in my mind into thoughts of my own.

If I write a recipe and you make it, then we are sharing both the words and the dish that results from them. Of course, you'll change the recipe. Of course, you'll hear the words differently in your head than I would in mine, but a connection is made nevertheless, and that connection is what writing recipes is all about.

When she was compiling the recipes that would eventually become *Mastering the Art of French Cooking*, Julia Child was living in France with her husband, Paul, who worked for the Office of Strategic Services (OSS), the agency that would eventually become the CIA. So it's not surprising that she maintained strict security about her recipes.

"Perhaps it was my old OSS training kicking in, or just my natural protectiveness," wrote Julia in her memoir, *My Life in France*. "But," she wrote in a letter to her sister, "the form we think is new, and certainly some of our explanations, such as that on our beloved mayonnaise, are personal discoveries." And so she sandwiched each recipe between pink sheets of paper on which she wrote "Confidential . . . to be kept under lock and key and never mentioned."

Since I learned to make mayonnaise at a very early age, I never thought of the technique as particularly secret. My mother and her seven siblings all learned it from their mother, and they in turn taught it to any members of my generation willing to learn. In our family, dishes like potato salad and Waldorf salad just had to be made with homemade mayonnaise. But some people feel just as strongly about certain brands of store-bought mayonnaise.

The novelist Tom Robbins is quite devoted to Best Foods–brand mayonnaise. "A lot of people in my hometown are loyal to Duke's," he says, "but I like Best Foods, which is the same thing as Hellmann's in the South." Robbins hails from Blowing Rock, North Carolina, and Duke's is made in Greenville, South Carolina. Hellmann's, which originated in New York City, was purchased by California-based Best Foods in 1932, and the two brands utilize the same formula and market it in similar packaging on their respective coasts.

In his 2003 novel, *Villa Incognito*, Robbins waxes poetic about mayonnaise. "Yellow as summer sunlight," he writes, "soft as young thighs, smooth as a Baptist preacher's rant, falsely innocent as a magician's handkerchief, mayonnaise will cloak a lettuce leaf, some shreds of cabbage, a few hunks of cold potato in the simplest splendor, restyling their dull character, making them lively and attractive again." The rave prompted many of his fans to start sending Robbins samples of their favorite brands of mayonnaise.

"There are some surprisingly good Mexican brands," says Robbins, "and the Japanese make extraordinary mayonnaise. I think I have about twenty-three brands in my refrigerator right now."

When Tom's wife, Alexa, invited my wife, Betsy, and me up to their place in La Conner for a private mayonnaise tasting, we hit the road with a few jars and bottles of our favorite brands. I also had, secreted away in a canvas shopping bag, a wire whisk, a deep mixing bowl, a fresh egg, a bottle of organic canola oil, some white balsamic vinegar, and a bottle of good Dijon mustard. It occurred to me that Tom and Alexa might like to learn how to make their own mayonnaise, and I wanted to see how the homemade stuff stood up in a taste test with the commercial brands, especially Robbins' beloved Best Foods.

But our evaluation of mayonnaises at Chez Robbins involved more than just the condiment itself. Mayonnaise is just one of the essential components of Robbins' favorite food, the tomato sandwich, a culinary delight he celebrated in his book of essays, *Wild Ducks Flying Backward*. In addition to various musings and critiques, the collection of stories and poems includes a piece called "Till Lunch Do Us Part," in which Robbins answers the age-old question, "What would you have for your last meal?" with an eloquent treatise on the tomato sandwich and its essential components, soft white bread and Best Foods mayonnaise. "But the mayonnaise would have to be the right mayo," Robbins reminds us. "The bread would have to be the correct bread. I don't want to leave the world on an inferior tomato sandwich."

So along with the various jars, tubes, and squeeze bottles of mayonnaise set out for our consideration, Alexa had acquired a soft and wonderful commercial white bread and several perfectly ripe red tomatoes. Then I pulled out my bag of tricks and went to work. But when I set about making a batch of homemade mayonnaise so that we could compare it to the store-bought stuff, Robbins did not appear to be interested. In fact, he seemed to deliberately avoid getting too close.

"I was occasionally watching you out of the corner of my eye," said Robbins later, "because I did find it interesting. But I didn't want to see exactly how it's made because I kind of like the idea of it being a mystery. I have been eating mayo for sixty years, and until ten years ago, I didn't even know what the ingredients are. I preferred to think of it as some kind of substance dug out of an underground cave in the French Alps.

"Socrates said, 'the unexamined life is not worth living,' but Oedipus Rex and I are not so sure. I like the mystery. I think Oedipus might have had a long and happy marriage with his mother if he hadn't found out the truth.

"I had a 1969 Mercury Montego, and in two hundred thousand miles, the head was never off the engine. I attribute that to the fact that I never once looked under the hood. I thought there was a ball of mystic light that kept the motor running.

"Beneath that silliness is a propensity for mystery. Every great work of art, whether it's a painting or a film, has an element of mystery. Mayonnaise is not a work of art, but it is the food of the gods; it is ambrosia.

"I have been quoted as saying that I don't know how to write a novel," he said, "and that was construed as a confession of incompetence. But that's not what I was saying. I'm saying I don't have a formula; I don't have a recipe for a novel." Rather, for Robbins, the creative process is something of a mystery. "I used to cook quite a bit, too," he said. "But I didn't use recipes. When I cooked, I cooked from vibration."

I like the idea of this well enough, and even though I write recipes for a living, I almost always cook without them, feeling my way from one step to the next. First this happens, then that happens. While the onions soften, I'm cutting the celery, and on a back burner, the rice is simmering away. But eventually, my left brain kicks in and I start to codify things because I want to share them. How much olive oil did I swirl into the pan? Was that a medium onion or a large one? Was it chopped or sliced? I like the geometric proof–like formula of a recipe, and I feel that if the precision of writing it down doesn't get in the way of the thing, it can be like an incantation, a magic formula for transforming a bunch of ingredients into something completely unlike its component parts. Mayonnaise is, after all, nothing like eggs and oil.

Making a recipe is not unlike making a sandwich. There is a formula, and when it is followed, real transformation occurs. That is magical.

HOMEMADE MAYONNAISE

Homemade mayonnaise is not only easy to make, it's also an exercise in practical magic. The end result is definitely greater than the sum of its parts. Many recipes, including some of mine, call for a food processor. But for a small batch of the stuff, especially someone's first batch, hand whisking is better. It helps to have a second pair of hands; one person handles the whisk and the bowl while the other person slowly dribbles in the oil. If white balsamic vinegar is not available, use white wine vinegar with a teaspoon of sugar.

1 egg
1 tablespoon white balsamic vinegar
1 tablespoon Dijon mustard
¾ teaspoon fine sea salt
1 ½ cups canola oil, preferably organic

◇ Whisk the egg in a medium mixing bowl with the vinegar, mustard, and salt until the mixture is very smooth, almost fluffy. Whisk for at least 1 full minute before adding any oil in order to set a good foundation.

◇ Whisk in a few drops of oil. Then, whisking all the while, build to a very slow but steady stream until all the oil is incorporated. As the sauce comes together to make a stable emulsion, the last of the oil can be added somewhat more steadily than the first few tentative dribbles.

Makes about 2 cups

A TOMATO SANDWICH

Tom Robbins claims that if he had the opportunity to request a last meal, his would be a tomato sandwich. Personally, I'm not sure what I would choose for a last meal, but I would like to have a tomato sandwich like this one from time to time. The sandwich always makes me think of Harriet the Spy, the eponymous character in the 1964 novel by Louise Fitzhugh. Harriet, who was raised almost entirely by her nanny, Ole Golly, was religious in her devotion to the tomato sandwich, which she ate every day for lunch. Like Robbins, she preferred her sandwich on white bread with mayonnaise.

2 slices soft white bread

2 tablespoons mayonnaise

2 or 3 slices from the center of a medium-size ripe red tomato

Kosher salt and freshly ground black pepper

◇ Spread one side of each slice of bread with a tablespoon of mayonnaise. Top one of the slices with the tomato, covering the bread in a single layer, then sprinkle with salt and pepper to taste. Plant the second slice of bread, mayonnaise-side down, on top of the tomatoes.

◇ Cut the sandwich in half and serve it at room temperature.

Makes 1 sandwich

BANANA PUDDING

"Time flies like an arrow; fruit flies like a banana."
—ATTRIBUTED TO GROUCHO MARX

For a time, I believed that the last thing my late brother Flip ever ate was a spoonful of banana pudding, when, in fact, it was a spoonful of peanut butter fudge. My brother was a chef and a painter whose culinary endeavors tended to steer clear of the housewifey types of dishes that involved boxed cookies and pudding mix, so I was baffled by the whole banana pudding thing. I am not entirely sure how I got the story wrong, but I can say that for as long as I believed that he had ended his culinary journey through life with a spoonful of banana pudding, I did not rest easy. Peanut butter fudge, with its hint of salt and its undertones of bitterness, is an old family favorite that I still make on occasion, and it seems like an acceptable last bite. But banana pudding would never do.

To my knowledge, my brother didn't even like banana pudding. Perhaps he had purchased too many bananas, I had mused. I suspect that having too many bananas is the only reason anyone ever makes banana pudding—even for those people who like banana pudding. It had seemed sad to me that Flip's last morsel of food would be a spoonful of something he made and ate just because he had to use it up.

Peanut butter fudge is a different story. This is something you make because you want to make it. Peanut butter never has to be used up the way ripening bananas do, and taking time to make peanut butter fudge is taking time to indulge yourself, to have some fun. It's an act of pure unadulterated pleasure, much more in keeping with my brother's character.

My second-oldest brother Flip was quieter than my other brothers. While the other two fought almost all the time, Flip stayed out of the fray and focused instead on reading science fiction and painting ships. He started painting at an early age and filled dozens of store-bought canvases. His early paintings were figurative, recognizable ships, like clippers and schooners, that cut through the storm-tossed waves of well-rendered oceans. Billowing sails were stark white against moonlit skies and ominous clouds. But over a period of years, his paintings grew more abstract, and the ships sailed out of sight.

The seascapes became increasingly intricate forays into fantastic, otherworldly realms, and more than one moon now occupied the skies. The colors ranged from brilliant turquoise and blood red to cobalt and emerald; the foregrounds were filled with hypnotic, hallucinogenic wonders. Eventually, he abandoned the small prefabricated canvases on which he learned to paint and worked on enormous canvases that he stretched himself over wooden frames that he built in his studio. Thousands of painstaking strokes in hundreds of colors came together in fantastic whirling images of mountains, clouds, and abstract forms that seemed vaguely reminiscent of people and animals. The paintings took months, even years, to complete.

In his formative years, Flip grew somewhat thoughtful, pensive, and removed. Even before he dropped out of high school and moved in with his friends, he would retreat to their garage apartments for weekends and indulge in psychedelic drugs. But when he was still at home, living with the family, he was an island of calm, a wellspring of understanding, and a kind of fortress for me and my other siblings. Each of us loved spending time with him, and I always felt safe, unjudged, and unperturbed in his presence.

One of Flip's crazier pursuits was playing the piano. This was crazy because he had never read music; nor did he have what most people would call an "ear for music." He was not one of those who could listen to a tune and reproduce it. Instead, he sat down at the piano and touched the keys in a random order that gradually unfolded into rhythms and melodies of his own devise, sounds that moved in chaotic and colorful patterns as dreamy as the waves and clouds that covered his increasingly abstract canvases. Long after he moved away from home, he would return to my parents' house late at night, after leaving the restaurant kitchen where he worked, and he would play my grandmother's upright piano in my mother's living room. It woke them up, my parents said, but it made them happy, too, to hear him back in their house playing the old piano.

Flip's own home didn't have a piano. Instead, it was mostly a studio filled with his enormous canvases and mobiles.

He learned to work a skill saw and cut fantastic crown moldings for his rooms. He crafted furniture from wood, items layered like works of art nouveau, with abstract shapes in place of flowers and leaves. Many of his works incorporated the lines of those sailing ships he painted when he was young. Some of his works were absurd; a pterodactyl-shaped mobile painted green and orange flapped its wings when you pulled a string. A hundred bleached wishbones salvaged from breasts of turkey that he roasted at the restaurant where he worked formed a lacy curtain hanging from the ceiling. Other works, like those fantastic landscapes on giant canvases, were almost sublime. He filled his house and his restaurant with art and laughter, reggae music and marijuana smoke, homemade jerk chicken and peanut butter fudge.

Then one day, before he set out on a fateful trip to rescue his dogs from the pound, where they had been interred for vagrancy, my brother made a batch of fudge. He sampled a spoonful from a corner of the platter on which it had been left to cool. After he got the dogs out of the hoosegow, he let them into the backseat of his old black Cadillac Seville, settled into the driver's seat, lit a cigarette, and died. The burned-out cigarette, with its undisturbed line of ash, was resting on the seat beside him. We took it as a reassuring sign that he did not struggle or clutch his chest in pain.

Shortly after my brother died, on the flight home from his funeral, I dreamed that my late grandfather was giving me a tour of the grand old hotel where he had worked before I was born. I was familiar enough with the hotel in my waking life, but mostly from the outside. It occupied an entire city block of my hometown before it fell into disrepair, standing empty for years before it was eventually torn down.

In my dream, I was thrilled that my grandfather was allowing me to see parts of the hotel I had only heard about. In real life, I had never been off the ground floor. Now I was to finally get a look inside the ballrooms. Up we went, climbing the Spanish-style wrought-iron staircase. Then we walked down the dark paneled halls. It was as beautiful as my mother had described it to me when I was a child. My grandfather, although he had died when I was an infant, seemed instantly familiar. He was overjoyed to have this opportunity to show me around, and he smiled a smile that made me feel completely welcome. "I want to see the kitchens," I said.

"Of course, of course," said my grandfather. He seemed to know all about my interest in cooking, and in a flash, I knew that he had been following my life and my career as long as I had lived. "But first," he said, "I have something else to show you." We were headed down one of the high-ceilinged hallways. The doors had those transom windows above, and I could hear music and laughter from the guest rooms. "Your brother's been painting," he said. He opened one of the doors. A vast room flooded with light was filled with colorful canvases, and though I couldn't see him, I knew my brother was there.

BANANAS FLIPPER

My brother's signature banana dessert was a far cry from banana pudding; it was something called "bananas Flipper," a playful variation on bananas Foster, the southern classic that was introduced at Brennan's Restaurant in New Orleans in 1951, before either of us was born. In its traditional form, bananas are sautéed in butter with brown sugar, rum, and banana liqueur. The flaming mixture is spooned over vanilla ice cream. To make his version, Flip fried a flour tortilla into the shape of a cup, sprinkled it with cinnamon and sugar, and filled it with Fosterian bananas. Here, to make things easier for the home cook and somewhat lighter for modern tastes, the flour tortilla is cut into thin strips and fried to make sopaipillas that serve as a crispy garnish; vanilla ice cream is replaced with coconut sorbet.

For the coconut sorbet

One 13.5-ounce can coconut milk

¾ cup water

¾ cup sugar

For the sopaipillas

2 tablespoons sugar

1 tablespoon cinnamon

Corn or canola oil, for frying

1 large flour tortilla

For the bananas

¼ cup unsalted butter

¾ cup brown sugar

1 teaspoon cinnamon

2 bananas, cut in half lengthwise, then split into thirds

1 tablespoon freshly squeezed lime juice

1 teaspoon vanilla extract

¼ cup dark rum

◇ To make the coconut sorbet, in a medium bowl, stir the coconut milk, water, and sugar together. Pour into an ice cream freezer and freeze until firm. Alternatively, fill a large mixing bowl with ice and salt and nestle a small saucepan in the ice; pour the coconut milk mixture into the saucepan and stir until it is soft-frozen. Transfer the sorbet to an airtight container and store in the freezer for at least an hour before serving.

◇ To make the sopaipillas, line a plate with a paper towel. In a small bowl, combine the sugar and cinnamon. In a heavy skillet over medium-high heat, or in a deep fryer, heat an inch of oil to 365°F. Cut the flour tortilla into quarters or strips. Fry the tortilla pieces, turning once until crisp and golden brown, about 4 minutes total. Drain them on the paper towel and, while they are still warm, sprinkle them with the sugar and cinnamon.

◇ To prepare the bananas and assemble the dessert, stir the butter with the brown sugar and cinnamon in a sauté pan over medium-high heat until the butter is melted. (The mixture will separate and the sugar will not melt completely, but forge ahead.) Gently sauté the banana pieces in the melted butter mixture until they are shiny, about 1 minute. Add the lime juice, vanilla, and rum, and swirl the pan until everything is well combined. If you are working over a gas burner, the rum may well catch on fire; if you are working over an electric burner, it probably won't, but if you want a dramatic show at the stove, you can light the fumes above the pan with a lighter or a match. Cook, rocking the pan gently until the flames go out, or until the alcohol has had a moment to evaporate, about 1 minute. Distribute the bananas and the sauce evenly among 4 serving dishes, plant a generous scoop of coconut sorbet in each dish, and top with a sopaipilla.

Makes 4 generous servings

MOM'S PEANUT BUTTER FUDGE

My mother's mid-twentieth-century aesthetic prompted her to keep a pantry well stocked with evaporated milk, which she called "canned cream." Her idea of good peanut butter was the "improved" kind that contained enough sugar and hydrogenated oil to prevent it from separating at room temperature. Influenced by the natural foods movement that swept the country during my formative years, I go for all-natural, preferably organic, peanut butter with no additives, and I am not partial to evaporated milk. Nevertheless, when all is said and done, my peanut butter fudge is almost indistinguishable from my mother's.

> 2 cups sugar, preferably organic evaporated cane juice
> 1 cup whole milk or evaporated milk
> 1 teaspoon kosher salt
> 1 cup peanut butter, preferably all-natural
> 2 tablespoons unsalted butter, plus more for buttering
> the baking dish
> 1 teaspoon vanilla extract

◇ Butter a 9-inch square glass baking dish (the fudge sets quickly, so you will need to have the dish ready in advance). In a deep saucepan over medium-high heat, cook the sugar and milk with the salt until the mixture reaches the soft-ball stage; this is the point at which a small spoonful of the mixture dropped into a glass of cold water forms a soft ball. It can be measured with a candy thermometer at about 240°F.

◇ As soon as the sugar mixture reaches the soft-ball stage, take it off the heat, and with a wooden spoon or a heatproof silicone spatula, stir in the peanut butter, butter, and vanilla. Continue stirring vigorously until the mixture begins to lose its gloss, about 2 minutes. Transfer the mixture quickly to the buttered baking dish and spread it in an even layer.

◇ Allow the fudge to cool completely, then cut it into 6 rows, and cut each row into 6 squares. Keep the fudge tightly wrapped to prevent it from drying out.

Makes 36 pieces

THE FOOD ESTABLISHMENT

"Generally speaking, the Food Establishment—which is not to be confused with the Restaurant Establishment, the Chef Establishment, the Food-Industry Establishment, the Gourmet Establishment, or the Wine Establishment—consists of those people who write about food or restaurants on a regular basis, either in books, magazines, or certain newspapers, and thus have the power to start trends and, in some cases, begin and end careers."

—NORA EPHRON

In the wake of Julia Child's success with *Mastering the Art of French Cooking* in the 1960s, cookbook editors and publishers launched an era of presenting American home cooks with a barrage of books that would afford us all an opportunity to prepare the "authentic" foods of every major culinary region of the world. Time Life gave us a whole series of works under the heading "Foods of the World." And to accomplish this monumental task, a small army of authors and consultants was drafted, including Mrs. Child herself and the already venerable M. F. K. Fisher, to produce the first volume, *The Cooking of Provincial France.* The team was drawn from a loosely organized cabal of cookbook authors that Nora Ephron, in her 1970 book *Wallflower at the Orgy,* called "the Food Establishment."

What this group of backbiting and authoritative individuals accomplished was to establish firmly in the minds of American cooks that there was a particular and authentic way to prepare any given dish. And while members of the establishment might argue among themselves about exactly which recipe for curry, or boeuf bourguignonne, or Greek dolmades was the be-all, end-all of its type, it was an unspoken given that such a Platonic ideal existed. Of course, it didn't.

Still, the notion that a Holy Grail version of every dish was out there somewhere, along with the equally dubious notion that an infallible prophet for every type of cuisine could be found, fueled the Food Establishment for decades. Knopf, the stable that produced Child, also delivered Madhur Jaffrey (the so-called Julia Child of Indian cooking), Marcella Hazan (a Julia Child of Italian cooking), and even Edna Lewis (a Julia Child of American soul food). These real authorities were supposed to lead us away from the sins of convenience promoted by the fictional characters from particular brands. "The most famous," writes Laura Shapiro in *Something from the Oven*, "was, and is, Betty Crocker, but she had many colleagues as self-assured and inventive as she was, including Mary Blake (for Carnation) and Carol Drake (for Safeway Stores)." Today, those fictional authorities are a little less self-assured than they used to be. Real, but somewhat contrived, personalities from the Food Network have taken their place and largely displaced the old Food Establishment as well. But members of the Old Guard still hold considerable sway. Among them is the indefatigable Diana Kennedy.

When she was in Seattle in 2008 to promote a new edition of her classic cookbook *The Art of Mexican Cooking*, she presented a cooking demonstration to a sold-out crowd at

Tom Douglas's Palace Ballroom. At age eighty-five, she was a formidable presence. Executive chef Eric Tanaka was on hand to assist her, and I was taking notes for an article for *The Seattle Times*.

"You should never use these yellow-brown onions," she told Tanaka. "They're too sweet. Use a medium white onion instead; it has much more onion flavor." Then she reached for a tomato.

"You want the whole tomato," she said, her punctuation very exact, still redolent of her English upbringing, even though she had lived in the United States and Mexico for more than half a century. "Use the skins, the seeds, the juice; don't do that French thing," she said, presumably referring to the French technique of cutting a peeled tomato into dice, discarding the seeds and pulp in the process. "It's ridiculous."

She moved on to serrano chiles, quartering them lengthwise and chopping them roughly. "If you have a book that tells you to remove the seeds and the white membrane from your chiles, then you know that the author doesn't know what the devil she's talking about and you can throw that book away."

"What is this?" she demanded when Tanaka passed her the ricotta cheese called for in the recipe she was making. "This is not ricotta; I don't know what this is. Ricotta— *requesón*—is what you get when you recook the whey left after making queso fresco. It's all in the book somewhere. You should read it. Honestly, I don't know how you people put up with the food you get in the shops. How do you put up with corn that's as sweet as custard?" she demanded of no one in particular. "How does this burner work?" she asked, and Tanaka took care of it.

"I might not know how to chop an onion or buy ricotta," said Tanaka good-naturedly, "but I do know how to light these burners." Tanaka, who picked up a James Beard Award in 2004 for Best Chef in the Pacific Northwest, knows more than he lets on.

"I don't mean to be so ornery," said Kennedy, "it's just part of my persona. *The New York Times* ran a story last week about how impossible I am, demanding authentic ingredients and things like that. But my stubborn nature sells a lot of cookbooks." Kennedy is indeed a stickler for authenticity. A recipe writer and cookbook author of uncommon precision, she is notoriously impatient with inferior ingredients and intolerant of shortcuts that undermine a dish's unique character.

"The first time I was in Seattle," she said, "it was 1956, and this was a real hick town. You couldn't get anything here. But now there's no excuse. There has been a complete and utter transformation and you can get absolutely anything here." Tanaka raised his shoulders in the universal gesture of uncertainty.

"Really," insisted Kennedy, "there is no excuse."

Kennedy's first trip to Seattle must have come shortly before she moved to Mexico in 1957 with her husband, Paul Kennedy, who was a foreign correspondent for *The New York Times*. After Paul died in 1967, the *Times* food editor, Craig Claiborne, persuaded Kennedy to start teaching classes on Mexican cooking in New York City. This led to several years of traveling throughout Mexico to research regional cooking there, and to her first book, *The Cuisines of Mexico*, in 1972.

At the Palace Ballroom in Seattle, Kennedy resigned herself to the state of the ricotta cheese and stirred it over a low flame. "Any Mexican cook will tell you that you will know when a dish is done because the food will tell you. There are no shortcuts."

"I finished a book recently on Oaxaca," she said. "And my editor wanted to know, 'Do you really have to include instructions on how to clean an iguana?' I said yes, of course I do."

"I just don't know what's happening to our food! But it's stupid, all this low-fat nonsense. Why would you want to cut out fat? What kind of person would want a boneless, skinless chicken breast when you could have a proper chicken?"

All this emphasis on authenticity has not gone unrewarded. For promoting understanding of Mexican culture in the English-speaking world, she was awarded status as a member of the Order of the British Empire by Queen Elizabeth II, and the government of Mexico has awarded Kennedy Order of the Aztec Eagle, the Mexican equivalent of knighthood.

By any measure, Diana Kennedy is an influential and authoritative woman. But most of the dishes in her books are relatively simple to prepare, as long as you follow her detailed instructions and take time to procure the right ingredients.

"The simplest food," writes Diana Kennedy in the updated version of *The Art of Mexican Cooking*, "is always the most difficult to prepare, for there are no predominant flavors to mask bad or indifferent ingredients or the careless handling of those ingredients."

Kennedy would undoubtedly be appalled by many of my attempts at Mexican food. I routinely put together a salsa composed largely of yellow onions, canned tomatoes, and dried jalapeños that have been reconstituted in some of the juice from the canned tomatoes. It's not that I don't know better—I have made wonderful salsas in Mexico using fresh white onion, fresh chiles, tomatoes, and lime—but I am comfortable adapting my techniques and even my tastes to what's most accessible where I live. When, during my college years, I worked at a Mexican restaurant, we transformed dried pintos into *frijoles refritos* every day, but at home, I'm at ease opening a can of refried beans and incorporating it into a burrito or a tostada. Sometimes home cooking is more about having fun and simply putting together something to eat than it is about being authentic.

But while I may have come to terms with the occasional can of refried beans, I am regularly conflicted about just how homemade a dish should be. I use canned coconut milk and a premade red curry paste to make a Thai-style curry dish. Does this make the dish less authentic than if I culled the coconut milk from fresh coconuts and made the curry paste myself with fresh chiles and herbs?

In her essay about the Food Establishment, Nora Ephron describes two wings, "each in mortal combat with the other." There are those she calls "revolutionaries," a group that tends to be "industry-minded and primarily concerned with the needs of the average housewife." Members of this group would advocate the use of canned coconut milk for sure. On the other side, there are "the purists or traditionalists, who see themselves as the last holdouts for haute cuisine." Although I tend to think of those traditionalists when I think of the establishment, I suppose both wings are still very much with us. Sandra Lee, with her *Semi-Homemade Cooking* show on the Food Network, would fall into the revolutionary camp; Naomi Duguid—who travels to the far corners of the earth to find out how indigenous people prepare dishes on their home turf, then provides detailed formulas for re-creating those dishes in North American kitchens—would qualify as a traditionalist.

In daily practice, I'm afraid that I might look more like one of the so-called revolutionaries, but my sympathies lie with the traditionalists. You might well find me attempting Duguid's Tibetan *momos* (steamed dumplings filled with lamb), but you'll never catch me making Sandra Lee's dreaded Kwanzaa Cake (a particularly abhorrent mess assembled from store-bought cake, canned frosting, and corn nuts). I certainly don't mind taking a few shortcuts when it comes to putting good-tasting, wholesome food on my family's table. Sometimes I'll go the extra mile and sometimes I won't; it just depends. Ultimately, it's about how interesting the process is and how delicious the results might be.

GUACAMOLE WITH FALL FRUITS

While I don't believe there is only one holy and authentic version of guacamole, I do think there is a best way to make it. In 2001, I was spellbound by a picture of Diana Kennedy's guacamole in an issue of Gourmet *magazine. My sister-in-law was on her way to Mexico at the time, and I asked her to bring me home a* molcajete, *a Mexican mortar and pestle made from lava rock. She delivered the* molcajete *in time for Thanksgiving, and since then, making the dip has become a part of our annual Thanksgiving Day routine. It's what we eat while the turkey roasts. (A recipe for this type of guacamole originally appeared in Kennedy's 1998 cookbook,* My Mexico.) *We serve the guacamole with store-bought tortilla chips, but if you want to be super authentic, you can fry your own from fresh tortillas.*

1 medium pomegranate

½ medium white onion, peeled and very finely chopped

3 serrano chiles, finely chopped

2 to 3 generous pinches kosher salt

4 large avocados

2 medium ripe pears, peeled and finely diced

2 tablespoons freshly squeezed lime juice

Sea salt

Tortilla chips, for serving

◇ To peel the pomegranate, fill a large bowl about two-thirds full with cool water. Score the pomegranate skin (avoid cutting too far into the flesh), then hold it under the water to break it in half. Set one half aside and, working under the water, peel the other half, allowing the good red arils, or seeds, to sink; the useless white pith will float to the top. Skim away the skin and pith and discard them. Pour off the water and reserve the seeds. (The pomegranate may be peeled several hours ahead of time and kept refrigerated until just before serving.)

◇ If one is available, use a *molcajete* (mortar and pestle) to crush the onion, chiles, and salt together to a paste. Alternatively, smash the onion, chiles, and salt with the side of a large knife on the cutting board.

◇ Cut the avocados into halves, discard the pits, and while the flesh is still contained in its cup of skin, cut a crisscross pattern in each half to produce 1-inch cubes. Use a large spoon to scoop the avocado dice from the skin. Stir the avocado cubes and the diced pear into the onion and chile mixture along with the lime juice. Season the dip to taste with sea salt. Stir half of the reserved pomegranate seeds into the guacamole and sprinkle the rest over the surface.

Makes about 4 cups

DEFINITELY NOT DIANA'S TURKEY TORTILLA SOUP

Tortilla soup is a fun family soup because each serving is assembled in the bowl. Chips, cheese, avocado chunks, and cilantro are stacked in the dish, then a ladle full of soup brings everything together. This version with its bright orange chunks of sweet potatoes—the kind usually called yams—is so colorful that it's sure to brighten everyone's day. Homemade turkey stock is so rich that it gels in the refrigerator; if it's unavailable, try enriching store-bought chicken broth with unflavored gelatin.

For the soup

> 2 tablespoons corn or canola oil
>
> 1 medium onion, peeled and thinly sliced
>
> 1 medium red bell pepper, cored and julienned
>
> 2 large poblano chiles or medium green bell peppers, cored and julienned
>
> 3 small sweet potatoes, peeled and cut into large matchsticks
>
> 2 tablespoons New Mexico–style chili powder
>
> 6 cups turkey or chicken broth, preferably homemade
>
> 2 envelopes unflavored gelatin (optional)
>
> 2 cups cooked turkey meat, shredded or cut into 1-inch pieces
>
> 2 teaspoons kosher salt

For the garnish

> Crisp, restaurant-style tortilla chips
>
> 4 ounces queso fresco, crumbled, or Monterey Jack cheese, grated
>
> 1 medium avocado, peeled and cut into ½-inch dice
>
> Cilantro sprigs, to taste
>
> 1 lime, cut into wedges

◇ In a large, heavy soup pot over medium-high heat, warm the oil and sauté the onion, red pepper, and chiles until the onion is softened and beginning to brown, about 5 minutes. Stir in the sweet potato matchsticks and sauté for about 1 minute longer.

◇ Stir in the chili powder, then add the turkey broth (if the broth is not homemade, stir in the gelatin). Bring the soup to a full, rolling boil. Reduce the heat to medium and stir in the turkey meat and salt. Simmer, uncovered, until the sweet potatoes are cooked through, about 15 minutes.

◇ While the soup is simmering, prepare the garnishes. Pile a few tortilla chips in the bottom of each serving bowl and put the rest in a separate bowl to be passed when the soup is served. Distribute the cheese and the avocado cubes evenly in little mounds in the center of each serving bowl, and plant sprigs of cilantro on top of the mounds.

◇ At the moment that everyone is ready to eat, ladle the hot soup over the garnishes in the bowls. Pass lime wedges and extra tortilla strips separately.

Makes 6 generous servings

CAFÉ MASALA

"Masala is the Hindi term for spice—not just the spice that one adds to food but also the spice of life, the excitement and vibrancy that come from stimulating conversation and a house full of friends and family."

—SUVIR SARAN

When I was serving as a chef instructor at Seattle Culinary Academy, I taught a class entitled Introduction to Restaurant Cooking. The course consisted of a theory class that covered the scientific and cultural context of five different world cuisines and a practicum that afforded students an opportunity to prepare dishes from those cuisines at an on-campus restaurant. To keep things interesting, I dabbled with various cuisines from quarter to quarter. Around a core trio of French, Italian, and Pacific Northwest cuisines, I threw in Spanish, Southeast Asian, Hawaiian, and Indian.

Since I am no authority on Indian cuisine, I had to invest considerable research into preparing the Indian menu for my class. A few weeks before I launched the new menu, I decided to call on a member of the Food Establishment, Madhur Jaffrey, who has authored some dozen books on Indian food for American cooks. I had met Jaffrey at a number of food-related conferences and sat with her once at a very long awards dinner, so I felt I knew her well enough to ask for help.

"Why don't you make the entire menu vegetarian?" she suggested. And, if I had not been required by the culinary college to teach certain competencies in handling meat and fish, I probably would have taken her up on that idea. On one level, her advice made perfect sense: the students needed to learn about vegetarian foods, and the Indian tradition was a perfect gateway to that kind of cooking. But since the students were required to learn core competencies—cooking animal protein among them—I could not include two weeks of only vegetarian dishes.

In the end, I had to compromise. For the core menu, I stuck with a series of non-vegetarian Indian dishes, but Jaffrey's advice inspired me to run a vegetarian special of the day, which I listed on the menu as "Today's Curry."

Like most people in the English-speaking world, I grew up believing that curry was a single thing, a stew made with a singular ingredient: curry powder. My mother's curry—a savory dish that filled the house with a wonderful smell—was always more or less the same. In fact, sameness was, as far as I was concerned, one of its virtues. I had the notion then (and still occasionally find my mind curling back into its old comfortable position) that every dish has a standard form—a Platonic ideal somewhere out there in the ether—and that as cooks, we strive to make our ingredients conform to that cosmological standard.

That is, of course, a lot of hooey. All dishes evolve and morph regularly into new dishes, and no family of dishes has done more of this ephemeral evolution than curries. As the editors of *Cook's Illustrated* magazine put it, "Almost any Indian stew can be called a curry."

But it came as quite a surprise to me when, at the age of ten or twelve, I learned that curry powder was, in fact, a blend of spices. I had imagined that curry powder was a thing in itself, and the discovery that it could be "made" by blending other spices prompted me to try to make my own. With the help of a friend's mother, I experimented with toasting some whole spices and grinding them into a fresh curry powder. Measured portions of coriander, cumin, turmeric, fenugreek, mustard seeds, and peppercorns went into a dry pan for toasting and then into a blender for grinding. Oh, the heavenly aromas!

I strove, of course, to make my spice blend taste and smell as much like the standard blend as I could. But the irony of what I was doing went right past me. Why seek out fresh, whole, individual spices and then try to make them taste exactly like a stale generic blend? In any event, I more or less succeeded and managed to make a curry powder that tasted just like the stuff in the can.

The whole notion of a standardized curry powder is completely alien to the great cuisine of India from which curry emerged. Attempts to reproduce and regulate the spice blends of the Indian kitchen came from Anglo-Indians who sought to reproduce the exotic flavors of India for the British cook. And in that way peculiar to the English, the notion of a correct, standardized curry emerged. According to Alan Davidson, the food historian who edited the *Oxford Companion to Food*, commercial curry powders have been available in England since the late eighteenth century, but they didn't come into vogue until somewhat later, during the Victorian era. Recognizing the disparity between Western curry powder and curry as it endures in India, Davidson concluded, "The whole curry powder scene is always going to be irreconcilable with its origins."

But in this century, cooks in the Western world have become somewhat more aware of the kaleidoscopic way in which spices can merge into any number of curry forms. It was Jaffrey who helped open my eyes at a cooking demonstration she gave years ago in Portland, Oregon. As she described the myriad blends of spices that can be used to season vegetables, stews, and grilled meats, Jaffrey talked about the various properties of spices that transcend the mere flavoring of food.

"In India," she explained, "we use spices almost like medicine." She rubbed a piece of turmeric between her fingers and invited us to do the same, drawing from sets of spice samples she had distributed before the class. "For example, turmeric has certain antiseptic properties, and it is traditionally rubbed onto fish before the fish is cooked. But there are other, more elusive ways that spices are used medicinally. We practice Ayurvedic medicine, which places a great deal of emphasis on hot and cold in the body. I remember that my grandmother would use a lot of ginger to warm herself."

Of course, all this was somewhat familiar to me. I had read Jaffrey's books, dabbled in Indian cooking at home, and gained as much as any American who has never visited India can: a basic understanding of Indian food. During the years I spent as a teenage vegetarian, Indian food was especially appealing to me because so much of it is vegetarian and because the basics are relatively easy to produce in any home kitchen.

Then Jaffrey explained how an Indian cook might select from a range of potential spice blends based not necessarily on some tradition or standard for what spices go with what foods, but on what spices seem appropriate to the way one is feeling. I filed this bit of information away and went about my business, but I started thinking about it again a few years later when a publisher sent me a review copy of a book by Jennifer Workman, *Stop Your Cravings: A Balanced Approach to Burning Fat, Increasing Energy, and Reducing Stress.*

A registered dietitian and sports therapist, Workman uses the principles of Ayurvedic medicine to show how "eating the right combination of foods and flavors can diminish cravings to the point that food is no longer an issue of stress and worry." She borrows the basic tenets of Ayurvedic medicine—including three basic body types and six basic flavors—to help readers shape a diet that matches their particular metabolic needs. I didn't have the patience to actually craft my own lifestyle according to her formula, but I did pick up one very useful bit of knowledge: full, bright flavors like the ones found in a good curry can satisfy hunger in ways that less flavorful foods never can.

Years later I had an opportunity to meet Indian cookbook author and restaurant consultant Suvir Saran, who was conducting a cooking demonstration at the Culinary Institute of America's Napa Valley campus. He brought home the notion that certain principles of Indian cooking, the authoritative use of spices and the resonance of food as medicine in the tradition of Ayurveda, are principles that deserve to be explored outside the realm of traditional Indian food. "There is no reason why these techniques can't be applied to chicken wings and meat loaf," he said.

So while I was teaching the Indian menu at Seattle Culinary Academy, I launched the section by bringing my students into the kitchen for a demonstration on cooking dal and making a flavorful sauté of aromatics known as a *tarka* to season it with. I introduced them to the basic notions of Ayurveda and explained that no matter what cuisine they chose to cook, these basic concepts could influence their cooking in a positive way by making them more sensitive to cooking simply, seasonally, and affordably. We almost intuitively understand, for example, that foods taste better when they are served in their own season. Who really wants watermelon or cucumber when it's cold outside? According to the principles of Ayurveda, these foods are "cooling" and should be eaten only when the weather is warm, but practically speaking, they are overpriced and less appealing when they are out of season. I would offer the same advice to home cooks trying to find simple, affordable, and flexible ways to feed themselves and their families.

Over the years, I have come to realize that some elements of Indian cooking belong in every cook's repertoire, regardless of what cuisine we are cooking. A blend of spices need not be a traditional or "authentic" curry blend in order to enliven a grilled piece of fish or a vegetable sauté. Understanding a *tarka*—which is made of onions, ginger, and garlic, and is used to add piquancy to a pot of dal in India—is as fundamental to modern American cooking—and every bit as vital—as a French mirepoix of carrot, celery, and onion.

GOLDEN CURRY POWDER

The cinnamon, cloves, and fennel in this spice blend lend sweet notes to the spices traditionally found in commercial curry powders. It's almost like a cross between Madras-style curry powder and the sweet-hot blend known as garam masala. Use the blend in Western-style curry dishes wherever curry powder is called for. The spice blend keeps, covered, in a cool, dark place for several weeks.

1 tablespoon coriander seeds
2 teaspoons cumin seeds
1 teaspoon fenugreek seeds
1 teaspoons peppercorns
1 teaspoon ground cardamom
1 tablespoon ground turmeric
2 teaspoons ground ginger
1 teaspoon cayenne pepper

◇ In a dry cast-iron skillet over medium-high heat, toast the coriander, cumin, fenugreek, and peppercorns for about 2 minutes, shaking the pan regularly, until the spices are very fragrant but not burned.

◇ Transfer the spices to a clean, dry mortar and pestle or a coffee grinder reserved for spices and grind until very fine. Stir or grind in the cardamom, turmeric, ginger, and cayenne just until blended.

Makes about ¼ cup

WEEKNIGHT VEGETABLE CURRY

If your pantry happens to hold canned coconut milk and garbanzo beans, this curry can come together in the time it takes to cook a pot of rice. The dish is inexpensive and it pleases a broad range of palates. It's also meat- and dairy-free. The combination of rice and garbanzo beans provides a complete protein, and the coconut milk makes it rich and creamy, so no one will miss the meat and dairy.

For the rice

3 cups water

2 cups basmati rice

For the curry

2 tablespoons coconut, corn, or canola oil

2 tablespoons Golden Curry Powder (page 153)

1 tablespoon turbinado sugar or brown sugar

1 tablespoon kosher salt

½ large onion, peeled and sliced

2 cups shredded kale, cabbage, or broccoli florets

2 large carrots, peeled and sliced

1 medium red bell pepper, cored and sliced

One 15-ounce can garbanzo beans, drained

One 13.5-ounce can coconut milk

⅓ cup dried Zante currants

1 small bunch green onions, thinly sliced

◇ To cook the rice, bring the water to a full, rolling boil over high heat in a medium saucepan with a tight-fitting lid. Stir in the rice, cover the pan, reduce the heat to low, and allow the grains to cook, undisturbed, for 20 minutes.

◇ To make the curry, warm the oil in a large skillet or wok over medium-high heat. Stir in the curry powder, sugar, and salt. Add the onion and stir-fry until it is tender and beginning to color, about 2 minutes. Stir in the cabbage, carrots, and red pepper; cook until the cabbage is wilted, about 2 minutes more.

◇ Stir in the garbanzo beans and coconut milk, reduce the heat to medium, and allow the curry to cook until the dish is heated through, about 3 minutes. Stir in the currants and green onions and serve the curry hot with the rice.

Makes 6 servings

RED LENTIL DAL

Dal, sometimes spelled dhal, is a generic name for the pulsed dishes that constitute the foundation of the Indian diet. Dal can be prepared in many ways. I like this version, which may not be particularly authentic but is a formula I have devised out of convenience. The lentils are cooked in water until tender; then the tarka—*a mixture of fried spices and onion—is stirred in at the end. With rice or bread, and a dollop of yogurt, the dal is a good vegetarian main dish, but it can also be served as a side dish with other curries.*

For the dal

6 cups water, plus more if needed

2 teaspoons kosher salt

2 bay leaves

2 cups red lentils

For the tarka

3 tablespoons ghee or canola oil

1 teaspoon mustard seeds

1 medium onion, peeled and thinly sliced

1 tablespoon finely chopped garlic

½ to 1 teaspoon dried red chile flakes

Plain whole milk yogurt, for garnish (optional)

◇ In a soup kettle over high heat, bring the water, salt, and bay leaves to a boil. Stir in the lentils. Reduce the heat to medium-low, cover, and cook for 30 minutes, or until the lentils are tender and beginning to disintegrate. While cooking, keep the lid of the pan slightly ajar to prevent the soup from boiling over.

◇ While the lentils are cooking, prepare the tarka. Heat the ghee in a sauté pan over medium-high heat, add the mustard seeds, and cook for a few seconds, just until they pop. Add the onion, garlic, and chile flakes to taste. Sauté for 5 minutes, or until the onion is soft and beginning to brown. Add the mixture to the cooked lentils.

◇ Cook the tarka and lentils together until the mixture has the consistency of a thick puree, about 10 to 15 minutes.

Makes 6 servings

IT'S A GOOD THING

"They say that nobody is perfect. Then they tell you practice makes perfect. I wish they'd make up their minds."

—WINSTON CHURCHILL

I realize at this late notice that the chances are quite remote and please forgive the seeming flakiness of the invite," wrote my normally very eloquent friend Dan Hinkley, apparently flustered at the keyboard. "Martha Stewart and her boyfriend, Charles Simonyi, are flying in (literally) for dinner on Saturday night with us at Windcliff. Due to the weather of last weekend, we are repeating our Hellebore Garden open on the same day, so our hands are full. Would there be any chance of you coming to whisk your magic in the kitchen and then you and your wife join us for dinner? We would hire your helpers and of course buy all food. Forgive me for such an awkward last minute invite (it is how the Martha machine operates), however, I thought that perhaps you might find it enjoyable and entertaining and we would love to have you back in our home."

Hinkley and his partner, Robert Jones, launched Heronswood Nursery in Kingston, Washington, and they live in nearby Indianola. Their home, Windcliff, is an incredible place. The kitchen is equipped with a black enameled Aga range, and windows from the kitchen open onto a spectacular view over their garden to Puget Sound and Seattle beyond. I had cooked there before, and I would have jumped at a chance to cook there again, with or without the reigning diva of domesticity. But cooking for Martha was certainly an added attraction. I was planning the menu before I even called Dan back.

Planning a menu—let alone cooking it—for Martha Stewart might seem like an intimidating challenge, and it was. I wanted everything to be impressive, but not overly thought out. In retrospect, I am surprised at how spontaneous it all turned out to be. I wanted to create the illusion that whatever I prepared was just what we would be cooking anyway. So my mind went first to what was on hand.

I had the better part of a case of Indian River Ruby Red grapefruit in my basement; they were at the peak of their season, and whenever they're in season, I tend to buy more than I really need. I also happened to have a rather large log of French white goat cheese in my refrigerator that a distributor had sent me as a sample. Years ago I worked for a chef who made a killer grapefruit and Belgian endive salad with goat cheese fritters, so almost as a reflex, I determined that that would be the first course.

In my cupboard was a bag of Anson Mills grits, which I happened to have because a flight attendant friend sometimes brings them to me when her travels take her down south. Based in Columbia, South Carolina, Anson Mills produces great milled products from organic heirloom grains. What goes with grits? Braised meat does; balsamic-braised short ribs leapt to mind. Of course, some Lacinato kale, prepared like Southern-style collards, would round out the plate. And after all that, a colorful array of tropical fruits on top of a crisp meringue would make a light but flavorful dessert. It would, after all, be Mardi Gras that weekend, so why not live it up?

I called Dan and told him that of course I would cook for Martha. Next, I called my butcher and ordered the short ribs, and then I arranged to have a few dozen Virginica oysters from Totten Inlet shipped over. And then I thought about Martha. If the old Food Establishment from the 1960s had sought to regenerate itself, it probably never would have elected Martha Stewart to its ranks. As much a lifestyle expert as a cook, Martha is just as likely to talk gardening or sewing as she is cooking or baking. Her area of expertise in the kitchen is not in any particular cuisine. Rather, her style of cooking is refined American. If she has a particular angle, it's perfectionism.

Stewart is such an American icon that I wonder if it is possible for anyone in this country to encounter her unencumbered by a bucket load of preconceptions. When she arrived, I made a conscious effort to approach her with what the Buddhists call a "beginner's mind"; that is, I wanted to be unprejudiced by anything I had heard or seen or read. In a way, I was successful. After meeting her, I see Martha in ways that I never did before. But I have to admit that when she shook my hand and said, "It's nice to see you," I felt as if I had known her for some time.

Martha is taller than some might imagine and, in her leather pants and crisp white shirt, she presented a striking figure. As my friend Donna, who was working the party as a server, put it, "She's hot!" At sixty-four, she was indeed beautiful in person. So I was staring and speaking a little slower than I normally do when I said, quite honestly, that I was thrilled to meet her.

Was I nervous about cooking for her? Of course. I had been from the moment I received that initial invitation. But standing beside me in the kitchen, slurping those ice-cold Virginica oysters almost as fast as I could shuck them—even picking up the oyster knife to shuck an oyster for herself—Martha put me immediately at ease.

"I'm easy to please," she assured me.

"Sure you are!" I said facetiously.

"I love everything. These oysters are fantastic. And the sausages!" Sizzling lengths of spicy andouille from Uli's Famous Sausages in Pike Place Market were being passed on trays.

And as she stooped over the Aga to inspect the braised short ribs, and helped me skim the fat off the top of the reducing cooking liquid, I felt as much at ease with her in the kitchen as I do with anyone. I always want for food to be as good as it can be, and I realized that I didn't want it any more or less because this was Martha.

As I contemplated over the days and weeks after cooking for her exactly why I respect this controversial American woman so much, it occurred to me that while many other American tycoons have made their fortunes off of resource extraction, Martha built her empire on information and education. What's more, the information she shared was something that no one else had properly valued—at least not for a long time. Tasks that had been undervalued, dismissed as "women's work," in decades past suddenly became meaningful when the authoritative Martha told us that they mattered. Whether it was organizing the linen closet, grooming the family pet, or baking perfect-looking cookies, Martha made it seem important and fun.

If Oprah Winfrey in her way persuades American viewers that we can "be our best selves," Martha Stewart convinces us to do our best work, even if we are simply making the bed or feeding the chickens. I respect that, and after cooking for Martha, I count myself one of her admirers.

BELGIAN ENDIVE AND GRAPEFRUIT SALAD WITH GOAT CHEESE FRITTERS

Worthy of a dinner party for Martha Stewart (when I served it to her, she ate every bite), this salad, adapted from my book Entertaining in the Northwest Style, *is also perfect for a family gathering.*

For the goat cheese fritters

One 11-ounce log soft white goat cheese

½ cup unbleached all-purpose flour

2 eggs

2 tablespoons water

½ cup bread crumbs or panko breading

1 teaspoon kosher salt

½ cup walnuts, finely chopped

Canola oil, for frying

For the salad

5 or 6 heads Belgian endive (5 large leaves per salad)

4 large red grapefruits

2 bunches watercress or 2 cups spinach, cut into fine ribbons

1 cup toasted walnuts

For the grapefruit vinaigrette

1 cup freshly squeezed grapefruit juice

2 tablespoons sugar

1 teaspoon kosher salt

½ teaspoon freshly ground black pepper

1 cup olive or walnut oil

◇ Prepare the fritters in advance. With a sharp knife dipped in hot water, cut the cheese into 8 rounds, each about ¾-inch thick. Line up 3 soup bowls; put the flour in one bowl; beat the eggs with the water in the second bowl; and put the bread crumbs, salt, and walnuts in the third bowl. Roll each piece of cheese in flour, shaking off the excess. Dip each flour-coated round of cheese into the egg mixture, then roll it in bread crumbs to coat it, and set aside. Fritters may be prepared ahead up to this point and refrigerated for several hours or overnight.

◊ Prepare the salad by trimming the base from each head of endive. Pull the larger individual leaves from each head, wash them, spin them dry with a salad spinner, and set aside (discard the cores or save them for another use). With a zester, remove the colorful outer rind from the grapefruits and reserve. With a sharp knife, cut the top and bottom from each grapefruit, then cut away the peel and remove any bits of white membrane left attached. Working over a bowl to catch the juice, remove each section by cutting along the membranes on either side. Cut in toward the center, then out. Sections may be prepared several hours in advance. Reserve the juice for the vinaigrette.

◊ Make the vinaigrette. Boil the grapefruit juice with the sugar, salt, and pepper in a nonreactive saucepan until it is reduced to ⅓ cup. Take the pan off the heat and whisk in the oil. Serve at once or cover and keep refrigerated until serving time.

◊ Arrange 5 leaves of endive in a palm-leaf pattern on each serving plate. Plant a section of grapefruit in each leaf and a bundle of watercress leaves at the base where the endive leaves meet.

◊ Just before serving, fry the goat cheese fritters. Heat ½ inch of oil to 375°F, or until a cube of bread dropped into the oil rises immediately to the surface and becomes golden brown in 1 minute. Fry the breaded cheese, 2 or 3 pieces at a time, for 2 minutes on each side, or until golden, and transfer directly from the hot oil to the plates, resting hot fritters on the beds of watercress. Drizzle each salad with the grapefruit vinaigrette and top with toasted walnuts. Serve at once.

Makes 8 servings

BALSAMIC-BRAISED BEEF SHORT RIBS WITH GRITS AND GREENS

Beef short ribs come in two forms: Korean-style "kalbi ribs" that have been sawed across the bones into ¼-inch-thick, quick-cooking steaks, and kosher-style 2-inch sections of rib (English-style ribs). These thick-cut ribs are chunkier and more suitable for braising.

For the ribs

    4 pounds beef short ribs, cut into 2-inch lengths and separated
        between the bones
    2 tablespoons kosher salt
    2 teaspoons cracked black peppercorns
    ¼ cup olive oil
    1 medium onion, peeled and thinly sliced
    4 cloves garlic, peeled and thinly sliced
    1 cup balsamic vinegar
    1 cup water
    1 bay leaf

For the grits

    3 cups water
    1 cup coarse-ground corn grits, such as Anson Mills brand
    ¼ cup (½ stick) unsalted butter

For the greens

    2 bunches Tuscan (Lacinato) kale, rinsed and drained
    ¼ cup extra-virgin olive oil
    4 cloves garlic, peeled and thinly sliced
    2 teaspoons kosher salt
    1 teaspoon freshly ground black pepper
    ¼ cup water

◇ Preheat the oven to 300°F. Pat the short ribs dry with paper towels and sprinkle them with salt and pepper. In a heavy Dutch oven or other covered, ovenproof pan over medium-high heat, warm the olive oil until it is shimmering, then add the short ribs and cook until the meat is well browned on top and bottom, about 4 minutes on each side.

◇ Transfer the ribs to a plate and hold them at room temperature. Sauté the onion and garlic in the pan drippings until the onion is soft and translucent, about 5 minutes.

◇ Stir in the balsamic vinegar, water, and bay leaf, and when the liquid is boiling, return the ribs to the pan. Cover and transfer the pan to the oven. Cook until the ribs are tender enough for the meat to come easily away from the bone, about 3 hours. When the ribs are tender, remove them from the braising liquid and keep them warm on a platter. Pour the pan juices into a deep saucepan, ladle off the excess fat that rises to the surface, then cook the juices over high heat until they are reduced to about half their original volume.

◇ About an hour before you plan to serve the ribs, start cooking the grits. In a large saucepan, bring the water to a full, rolling boil and whisk in the grits. Cook, stirring vigorously for a few minutes until the grains begin to swell and thicken. Reduce the heat to low, cover the pan, and simmer the grits gently until they are very soft, about 45 minutes. Just before serving the grits, stir in the butter.

◇ To prepare the greens, strip the tender sides of the leaves away from the tough stems and discard the stems. Working with 2 or 3 leaves at a time, roll the leaves into bundles and cut across the bundles to make thin ribbons of the greens. Warm the oil in a large sauté pan over medium-high heat, stir in the garlic, salt, and pepper. Immediately toss in the greens and cook, keeping them in constant motion with a pair of tongs until they are lightly coated with the oil and beginning to wilt, about 3 minutes. Add the water to one side of the pan, taking care to avoid getting splattered, and continue cooking and stirring the greens around until they are tender, about 2 minutes more.

◇ Put a dollop of grits on each plate. Distribute the ribs evenly among the plates, propping them against the grits, then plant a mound of the greens at the junction of the grits and the ribs. Finally, ladle a generous portion of the reduced pan juices over each serving of ribs.

Makes 8 servings

CRISP MERINGUES WITH EXOTIC FRUITS

Crisp meringues provide the foundation for several classic desserts. Here, they are topped with a buttery "curd" or fruit preserve and a variety of fresh fruits. Curd is a form of fruit spread usually made with citrus fruits, but passion fruit makes a wonderful variation. Since the meringues can be baked well in advance and the curd can be prepared ahead of time and kept refrigerated for several days, this makes a great dessert for a special dinner when you want the security of having everything set in advance. If passion fruit puree is unavailable, use freshly squeezed lime juice with a teaspoon of freshly grated lime zest to make a lime curd instead.

For the meringues

¾ cup sugar

¼ cup powdered sugar

½ cup (about 4 large) egg whites

1 teaspoon freshly squeezed lime juice

¼ teaspoon kosher salt

For the curd

½ cup passion fruit puree

6 tablespoons (¾ stick) unsalted butter

4 egg yolks

⅔ cup sugar

For the garnish

A variety of colorful tropical fruits, such as kiwi, mango, and blood orange, chopped into bite-size pieces

◇ To prepare the meringues, line 2 baking sheets with parchment and preheat the oven to 225°F. Whisk together the two sugars and set aside.

◇ In the bowl of an upright electric mixer, whip the egg whites with the lime juice and salt until the whites are very foamy and just beginning to hold soft peaks, about 2 minutes. Very slowly stream in half of the sugar mixture and continue whipping until the egg whites hold stiff peaks and become very smooth and glossy, about 2 minutes more.

◇ With a rubber spatula, fold the remaining sugar into the whipped egg whites, then pile the mixture into a 1-gallon ziplock bag. With scissors, snip off about ½ inch from one corner of the bag to create a pastry bag. Pipe the meringue through the impromptu pastry bag onto the lined baking sheets, forming 12 whirled 5-inch circles.

◇ Bake the meringues until very crisp and dry, about 3½ hours. The meringues may be baked several days ahead and kept in an airtight container in a cool, dry place.

◇ To make the curd, put the passion fruit puree and the butter in a large nonreactive saucepan with a very heavy base. Cook over medium heat until the butter is melted. Meanwhile, whisk the egg yolks and sugar in a mixing bowl until light and fluffy, about 3 minutes. Stir ½ cup of the hot passion fruit mixture into the egg yolks, then add the yolks to the pan with the passion fruit puree and cook, stirring constantly, until the mixture has thickened and is steaming hot, about 5 minutes. Transfer the cooked curd back to the mixing bowl and chill completely before using.

◇ To assemble the desserts, put a crisp meringue in the middle of each dessert plate, top it with a ¼-cup dollop of the passion fruit curd. Arrange slices of the fruits on top of the curd and serve at once.

Makes twelve 5-inch meringues

PASTURE PERFECT

"A chicken in every pot and a car in every garage."
—HERBERT HOOVER

U nlike some twenty-first-century do-it-yourselfers, I have never endeavored to keep my own chickens. This doesn't mean that I won't someday, but so far, I'm just not ready to make that commitment. I am, however, extremely uneasy about buying chicken from the grocery store. (I'm not saying I never buy those birds; I'm just saying I don't feel at ease with it.)

When I buy a chicken in the grocery store, I only buy birds bearing labels like "certified organic" and "free range," but those labels have ceased to persuade me that the bird in the bag has led anything but the most dreadful life imaginable. I hate having to say it, but it's true. Even when they're free of antibiotics—and organic birds are, by law, raised without antibiotics and growth hormones—battery-farmed animals lead wretched lives. USDA standards for birds labeled "free range" require that the birds have access to the outdoors, but what that means is fairly vague, and there are no minimum guidelines for how much space the birds are allowed in which to "range." Typically those birds are still raised in a method characterized within the industry as "high-density floor confinement."

The alternative—buying a pasture-raised bird from a farmer I know—sometimes seems almost prohibitively expensive, but it's worth it. Joel Salatin of Polyface Farm, a self-proclaimed grass farmer who has become a spokesperson for a healthier and more humane way of raising poultry, prefers the term "pastured poultry" for his birds—not a legal definition, just an apt one. The description also applies to birds raised by my friends George and Eiko Vojkovich, who own Skagit River Ranch in Sedro-Woolley, Washington.

They raise chickens for eggs and meat, as well as pigs and cattle for pork and beef. I have visited their farms any number of times over the years. I have been there when the chickens were being "processed," and while I feel a certain amount of shame whenever I eat animals raised in the confinement of modern factory farms, I feel completely comfortable and even somewhat proud of eating animals raised by George and Eiko in the open air the way these animals are. And when you get a bird like this in your kitchen, you really don't want to mess it up. I like to prepare a classic like coq au vin and serve it with spinach noodles made from pastured eggs.

"Coq au vin" translates to "rooster with wine," and originally the dish took advantage of the tenderizing effects of wine to render a tough old rooster easier to eat. But the wisdom of modern farming has deemed that, except for the occasional male left around to fertilize the eggs, all chickens should be female. (This is true even on farms that practice humane and relatively sustainable practices because they purchase their chicks from large-scale breeders.) Chickens are sexed almost as soon as they hatch, and males are immediately discarded, so roosters are hard to come by.

It may soothe the stickler to note that the same is true in France, where this dish originated. Even there, hens are considered more tender and flavorful than their suitors, and home cooks and restaurant chefs alike routinely prepare female birds in the manner devised for cooking roosters.

Once, I did have an opportunity to eat true coq au vin. Some friends of mine used to keep a little flock of chickens for the eggs, and they kept a rooster just to make the little flock complete. But the randy old fellow was troublesome; he exhausted his harem, attacking them with disturbingly brute force, and even charging unwitting people who dared to walk through his yard. Eventually it was determined that he should be dealt with in the form of a stew. A large bottle of red wine and a pound of bacon were ordered up, and the bad-tempered bird was summarily dispatched by means of a hatchet that was ordinarily reserved for splitting kindling wood.

At the time, I thought the whole situation was somewhat barbaric. I followed the ovo-lacto regimen popular in the late seventies that embraced milk and eggs but not meat, and I considered myself a vegetarian. But the animals weren't mine, and I felt I had no say in the sentencing of the rooster. So when I was invited to dinner and discovered that the pièce de résistance was the old rooster that I had occasionally chased away on my way to gather eggs in my neighbors' henhouse, I was a little squeamish. Initially I declined the offer of the stew.

"Oh, no thanks," I said. "I don't eat meat." I helped myself to some of the buttered noodles with parsley and resigned myself to what looked like a rather one-dimensional repast.

"It's not really meat," insisted my friends. "It's a bird, not a mammal. And besides, you've eaten the eggs he fertilized." They had a point. And the stew smelled terrific.

"It has bacon," I protested.

"Oh, go ahead," said the host. And he put a spoonful of the steaming stuff on my plate. Mushrooms, pearl onions, and a purple sauce surrounded the wedge of potentially offending flesh. I surrendered. Okay, I thought, now I eat birds, and a little bacon. I had to admit that the coq au vin was delicious. It was, in fact, the best thing I had eaten in a long, long time.

Since then, I have cooked a number of chickens in wine, but I seldom follow the classic Burgundian formula for coq au vin, which calls for an overnight soak in red wine. This step is unnecessary with tender chicken, anyway. And ever since I discovered the variation devised in Alsace for coq au Riesling, I have all but abandoned the red wine version and adopted my take on an Alsatian version of the dish as my own American original.

With the chicken, I like to serve noodles, and if I have the time and inclination, I make the noodles myself, preferably utilizing eggs from the same farm where I got the chicken. If I have planned ahead and the stars are all lined up correctly, I can even pull off a batch of homemade spinach pasta to serve with the dish. The chicken, after all, has to braise for a while, and the cook needs something to do while the chicken is cooking, so why not roll up your sleeves and make some spinach noodles?

POULET AU RIESLING

Made with fresh-tasting white wine instead of the traditional red, this chicken cooked in wine bears some allegiance to coq au vin, but comes together far more quickly and seems somehow more suited to contemporary tastes. Instead of the usual button mushrooms, I use forest mushrooms like chanterelles, shiitakes, or morels, depending on the season. And I always begin with a free-range or organic chicken. Begin with a whole chicken and cut it into 8 pieces, or buy 4 pounds of bone-in thighs and drumsticks.

¼ cup (½ stick) unsalted butter

1 tablespoon olive oil

¼ pound (about 4 thick slices) bacon or pancetta

4 pounds bone-in chicken thighs and drumsticks, or 1 cut-up chicken

1 tablespoon kosher salt

1 teaspoon freshly ground black pepper

¼ teaspoon freshly ground nutmeg

2 medium onions, peeled and chopped

3 or 4 cloves garlic, peeled and thinly sliced

½ pound forest mushrooms, sliced fairly thin

3 cups Riesling

1 cup heavy cream, preferably organic

3 tablespoons chopped parsley

◇ In a heavy 1-gallon stockpot or Dutch oven over medium-high heat, melt the butter with the oil. Cut the bacon into ½-inch pieces and cook them until they are crisp. Lift the bacon pieces out of the pan with a slotted spoon and set aside on a plate lined with a paper towel.

◇ Sprinkle the chicken pieces with the salt, pepper, and nutmeg and arrange them skin-side down in the pan. Brown the chicken pieces on both sides, about 5 minutes per side. When the pieces are browned, lift them out of the pan and set aside on a plate. Pour off and discard all but about 4 tablespoons of the fat. Reduce the heat to medium and sauté the onions and garlic in the hot fat left behind. Cook, stirring, until the onions have softened but have not browned, about 3 minutes.

◇ Add the mushrooms and continue cooking until they are heated through, about 3 minutes. Raise the heat to high, pour in the Riesling, and when the wine comes to a full, rolling boil, put the chicken pieces back into the pot. Turn the heat down to medium-low and simmer gently, uncovered, until the chicken is cooked through, about 30 minutes.

◇ Lift the chicken pieces out of the pan and return them to the plate. Pour in the cream and boil the sauce until it is reduced by two-thirds and is beginning to thicken. Return the chicken to the pan along with any juices that have accumulated on the plate. Sprinkle with the bacon pieces and parsley and serve hot with Pâtes Vertes (opposite page) on the side.

Makes 4 to 6 servings

PÂTES VERTES (SPINACH NOODLES)

One year, when I was living near some laying hens and planting more spinach than I could eat, I decided to try making spinach pasta. In other, less abundant, years, I discovered that even frozen spinach works beautifully in this dish. The key is to cook the spinach first, squeeze out as much of the excess water as you can, and chop the spinach very, very fine. The dough comes together in minutes, either on a cutting board or in a food processor. Rolling out the dough by hand is not a big deal if you have enough counter space, but if you have a pasta maker, it's easier.

1 pound fresh spinach, or one 10-ounce package frozen spinach

1 egg plus 1 egg yolk, lightly beaten

1 ½ cups unbleached all-purpose flour, plus additional as needed

2 tablespoons kosher salt

¼ cup (½ stick) unsalted butter

Freshly ground black pepper

◇ If you're starting with fresh spinach, remove all the stems and rinse the leaves in a sink full of cold water. Lift the leaves out of the water, transfer them into a salad spinner, and spin off the excess water. If you're using frozen spinach, thaw it first and then proceed. Cook the spinach in a dry saucepan until it releases its own liquid, and continue cooking and stirring until the leaves are wilted, about 4 minutes. Take the spinach off the heat, and when it is cool enough to handle, squeeze out as much of the liquid as you can.

◇ Put 1 cup of the flour into the work bowl of a food processor and, with the motor running, add the beaten egg and spinach. Pulse the motor off and on until the mixture comes together to form a sticky dough, then continue adding flour a few tablespoons at a time, pulsing the motor off and on until the sticky paste forms a ball that leaves the sides of the work bowl. (Alternatively, finely chop the cooked spinach. Pile 1 generous cup of flour in a mound on a clean kitchen counter. Press a depression in the center of the mound to create a small well, then put the beaten egg and spinach into the well and beat them with a fork, gradually working in the surrounding flour. Knead in enough additional flour to create a fairly firm dough.)

◇ On a lightly floured surface, knead the dough until it is very smooth and very springy, about 5 minutes. Wrap the dough in plastic wrap or a damp, lint-free towel and leave it alone for at least 10 minutes; this will allow the gluten that was developed during the kneading process to relax so that the dough can be rolled out.

◇ Clean and dry the work surface then sprinkle it with flour. Roll the pasta into a large circle about ⅛-inch thick. Working quickly to prevent the pasta from drying out, elongate the circle of dough into a rectangle by stretching it as you roll. Continuing to work quickly, roll and stretch the pasta until it is as thin as you can get it. You should have a rectangular sheet of pasta dough about 24 inches long and 18 inches wide.

◇ To cut the noodles, dust the sheet of dough with a little more flour, then roll it like a jelly roll and cut across the roll to make ribbons about ¼-inch wide. Unfurl the ribbons of pasta as soon as they are cut so that they don't stick together, and sprinkle with a little more flour as needed.

◇ To cook the noodles, put 1 gallon water and the salt in a large stockpot over high heat. When the water comes to a full, rolling boil, stir in the noodles. Stir attentively to prevent the noodles from sticking together. As soon as the water returns to a boil, count to 10 and test the noodles; cook until they are just tender.

◇ Drain the noodles through a colander, reserving about ½ cup of the cooking water to toss with the noodles later. Put the butter into the empty pot and stir it around until it is mostly melted. Add the cooked noodles to the pan and toss with the hot butter. Stir in enough of the cooking liquid, 1 tablespoon at a time, to make a creamy sauce around the noodles. Season to taste with salt and pepper and serve hot.

Makes about 1 pound pasta, serving 4 to 6

RUMAKI

*"Food is the mainstay of any party, be it a cocktail party,
a tea, a barbecue, or just a plain brawl. It doesn't have
to be fancy, but it must be good."*

—TRADER VIC

A few years ago, for reasons I cannot explain, I was stricken with an urge to make rumaki. The peculiar combination of chicken liver and water chestnuts wrapped in bacon was once the quintessential element of every mainland luau, and every faux-Hawaiian pupu platter. When I was the chef at Seattle's Canlis Restaurant, a few old-timers would occasionally request rumaki because they had enjoyed it there decades earlier and wanted to relive some happy memory. But rumaki played no part in my own happy memories; my urge to make and eat the dish seemed absurd. I thought it would pass and I tried to ignore it, but the craving lingered on the periphery of my consciousness for months.

Then I went to visit my father in Florida, and out of the blue, he offered me his faded copy of *Trader Vic's Book of Food and Drink*. The signed first edition of the 1946 classic was a souvenir from Pop's navy days, something he'd picked up on shore leave in Oakland in 1948. This was the affirmation I needed. I was going to make the rumaki.

"Trader Vic himself signed it," said Pop. "It was the first time I ever had a book signed by the author. I think you should have it." I thought so, too. As soon as Pop handed me the book, I flipped immediately to the index, sure I would find rumaki, but it wasn't there.

Vic—also known as Victor Jules Bergeron Jr., the proprietor of a hangout in Berkeley known as Hinky Dinks—is generally credited with the invention of this distinctive appetizer. Chock-full of Polynesian paraphernalia, the restaurant waxed by the 1960s into a chain of twenty-plus Trader Vic's restaurants in North America, Europe, and Asia. As tiki-mania waned in the eighties and nineties, some of the restaurants were shuttered, including the one at Seattle's Westin Hotel, which closed its carved wooden doors in 1991. After the turn of the century, nostalgia for all things faux-Polynesian prompted a resurgence of Trader Vic's restaurants opening or reopening in cities from Dallas to Dubai.

Recipe or no, the Trader Vic cookbook had inspired me. Pop was going to visit me in Seattle in a few months, and I planned on shaking up some mai tais and making some rumaki to share. My local grocery store stocks excellent chicken livers from organically fed chickens, and I had a stash of great bacon from a pig farmer in Skagit Valley. I had never worked with fresh water chestnuts, but I knew that canned simply wouldn't do. So I made a pilgrimage to Viet Wah

Supermarket, a big Asian grocery on South Jackson Street in Seattle's Little Saigon neighborhood.

The Chinese water chestnut (*Eleocharis dulcis*) is a corm found at the base of the stem of a water-loving sedge plant. A corm is an underground stem base of a plant that is sometimes mistakenly called a bulb. Unlike a bulb, though, the interior structure of a corm is not layered; it's starchy like a tuber.

"These are very good," promised the grocer at Viet Wah. She seemed genuinely excited that I was buying them. The bag contained several dozen wooden-looking beads, each one roughly the size of a walnut. "You cook them in stir-fries, nice and crunchy, really delicious."

With the exotic corms safely in hand, I was good to go. But without a recipe, I had to wing it. I pared the water chestnuts; marinated some chicken livers in soy sauce spiked with sherry, brown sugar, and ginger; wrapped everything in partially cooked bacon; and held the rumaki fast with bamboo picks. Then I dispatched them to the oven, where the bacon crisped and the livers grew firm. The water chestnuts themselves were sweet and crunchy, not unlike jicama. The marinated livers were tender and meaty and the bacon was . . . well, it was bacon. The tidbits were indescribably delicious.

Not long after my father and I enjoyed rumaki in Seattle, I went to visit my son in Ohio, where he was enrolled as a freshman at Oberlin College. During the course of the visit, we went into a used bookstore, and there, I came across a copy of *Trader Vic's Pacific Island Cookbook*, a colorful 1968 sequel to the book my father had given me. I flipped to the index, and, sure enough, there was the formula for rumaki.

Considerably more complicated than my improvised version, it listed garlic and bay leaves, star anise, and cinnamon sticks among the ingredients; the cooking process was more demanding, too. Forget it. I'm sticking with my own improvised version.

TWENTY-FIRST-CENTURY RUMAKI

A streamlined version of the mid-century pupu platter staple, this rumaki relies on fresh water chestnuts instead of canned. Serve these puppies with mai tais, or, if you're like my father, Scotch on the rocks.

¼ cup soy sauce

2 tablespoons dry sherry

1 teaspoon freshly grated ginger root

1 teaspoon brown sugar

12 ounces chicken livers

12 slices bacon, cut in half

24 whole fresh water chestnuts, peeled

24 toothpicks

◇ Combine the soy sauce, sherry, ginger, and brown sugar in a small bowl. Trim the chicken livers of any sinews and cut them into 24 pieces, each ½ ounce. Place the chicken livers in the small bowl with the soy sauce mixture and marinate in the refrigerator for 30 minutes.

◇ Preheat the oven to 450°F. Set a cooling rack over a brown paper bag or a few layers of paper towels. Spread the bacon on a baking sheet and cook until the bacon is translucent and sizzling, but not yet crisp, about 7 minutes. Take the bacon out of the oven and drain the pieces on the prepared cooling rack.

◇ After the chicken livers have marinated and the bacon has been partially cooked, assemble the rumaki. Distribute the marinated liver pieces and the peeled water chestnuts evenly among the bacon pieces and, working with one piece at a time, wrap the bacon strips around the livers and chestnuts, securing each bundle with a toothpick.

◇ Place the rumaki on a broiler pan and bake on the uppermost rack of the oven until the bacon is crisp, about 15 minutes. Serve hot.

Makes 24 bite-size appetizers

MODERN MAI TAI

The mark of the modern bar, aside from an array of obscure brands of liquor that most people have never heard of, is a selection of syrups and infusions handcrafted by the bartender on site. Crafting these tinctures at home can be fun. They hold up well in the refrigerator and make good non-alcoholic sodas, too. (Just put an ounce or two of a good flavored syrup in a glass and top it off with carbonated water.) Try forgoing the traditional commercially produced grenadine, making your own pomegranate syrup instead, and suddenly you'll see the mai tai in a new light. Orgeat is an almond syrup that can be purchased in the form used to flavor coffee drinks, but if you don't want a quart of the stuff, making your own with almond extract is a cinch. You can even make your own orange liqueur by infusing grain alcohol with orange zest for a couple of weeks and sweetening it to taste.

For the pomegranate syrup

1 cup pure pomegranate juice

1 cup sugar, preferably organic evaporated cane juice

For the orgeat syrup

1 cup water

1 cup sugar, preferably organic evaporated cane juice

½ to 1 teaspoon natural almond extract

For the cocktails

2 ounces dark rum

2 ounces light rum

1 ounce clear orange liqueur, such as curaçao

1 ounce pomegranate syrup or grenadine

1 ounce orgeat syrup

¼ cup freshly squeezed lime juice

Lime zest or slices, for garnish

◇ To make the pomegranate syrup, boil the pomegranate juice and sugar in a small saucepan, stirring occasionally, until the sugar is dissolved. Transfer the liquid to a jar with a close-fitting lid and store it in the refrigerator for up to 2 weeks.

◇ To make the orgeat syrup, boil the water and sugar in a small saucepan until the sugar is dissolved. Stir in the almond extract to taste. Transfer the liquid to a jar with a close-fitting lid and store it in the refrigerator for up to 2 weeks.

◇ To mix the drinks, put the dark rum, light rum, orange liqueur, pomegranate syrup, orgeat syrup, and lime juice in a cocktail shaker and top it off with ice. Give the shaker 6 or 7 swift shakes, then strain the contents into 2 old-fashioned glasses filled with fresh ice cubes. Decorate each drink with a twist of lime zest or a slice of lime.

Makes 2 drinks

SCHOOL LUNCH

"Be polite to your servers; practice saying 'Thank you!'
Sit with your class; do not move around.
Always eat sitting down.
Clean up after yourself.
Put trays, garbage, silverware, etc., in the appropriate places.
Always use appropriate language and topic of conversation, or be
prepared to eat by yourself. (This includes not making rude noises.)
As soon as you are finished and excused, you may go to the
playground for recess."

—LUNCHROOM RULES, CHIMACUM SCHOOL DISTRICT, 2010

I was working as a full-time dinner chef for most of the years my sons were young, and my kids were usually in bed before I got home from work. And before I was fully awake, they were on their way to school again. So, in order to spend a little quality time with them, I sometimes met them in their school cafeteria for lunch.

When they were in elementary school, this was no big deal. My younger son, especially, was thrilled to see me, and so, for the most part, were his friends. "Erich! Your dad's here!" they'd squeal. They were all eager to tell me about their morning, quick to recommend the fish-shaped fritters or the fresh fruit. They warned me about what to avoid—mini-burgers—and what to eat first—the rapidly melting frozen yogurt bars. Erich loved this; when Dad was at school, he was a star.

But by the time they reached middle school, the thrill of having me there was gone, and the guys were consistently bringing lunches I packed at home. I remember a particular visit when my older son was going into seventh grade—having one of my weird homemade lunches was challenging enough; having me there in the flesh was worse. I think most kids, especially after they reach age ten or so, manage to create the illusion, at least among their peers, that they are independent creatures. They remind me of house cats, refusing to acknowledge that their human keepers are anything other than servants. My appearance in the lunchroom blew his cover.

My sons may have seen their homemade lunches as weird, but lunches made in school cafeterias are weird, too. It varies from district to district and from state to state, and certainly from decade to decade, but school lunch is universally strange. On the Gulf Coast in the 1960s, it had its own peculiar kind of strangeness. Mashed potatoes, which were ubiquitous, were always served from an ice cream scoop. Fruit was in the form of a "cocktail"—cubes of peach and pear and orbs of grape that had all been rendered the same pale gray-green by long confinement in a can. Meats, usually ground, were cooked in a reddish sauce that wavered indecisively between country gravy, marinara, and barbecue. Still, a kid could always count on hot rolls and cold milk; lactose intolerance and wheat allergies were unheard of in those days.

Today, there are choices. A kid can actually opt for a bean burrito or a burger. Pizza is a common choice. The packaging and branding seem weird to me, as if the kids were going out for fast food instead of eating at school. But there is an honest-to-God fresh green salad every day—granted, it's just some very wet iceberg lettuce with some kind of milky dressing, but it's salad nonetheless. And the fruit is real grapes and real apples, not canned fruit cocktail.

Occasionally, when we would complain about how gruesome school lunch was, my mom would get creative and make our lunches. This meant bologna on spongy white bread, or peanut butter on spongy brown bread, plus a banana or an apple and a dime for milk money. The sandwich and fruit were packed not in the proverbial brown bag, but in a themed lunch box. My favorite was "The Man from U.N.C.L.E."

One August, Mom determined that all of us should carry widemouthed insulated thermos bottles inside our lunch boxes. In the midst of our back-to-school shopping, she bought one of these things for each of us. The thermos jars were decorated, as I recall, in an amber and orange plaid design—the ugliest-looking things I had ever seen. The noble plan was that these thermoses would be filled with something hot and nourishing, like soup or leftover spaghetti from the night before. Hatched, perhaps, over the bridge table with the other moms, or pulled fully blown out of some women's magazine, this scheme quickly went awry.

In early October, Mom sent me off with a thermos bottle full of leftover chili. It was so utterly outré. I was twelve at the time, that age when identity is associated with all sorts of things, that age when one would never be caught dead eating something like chili from a thermos bottle. I opened the thermos bottle and globbed some of the stuff into the little plastic dish that came with the bottle.

"What is that?" screamed a girl from across the table.

"I think it's chili," I answered humbly.

"Gross," came the consensus.

I ate the saltine crackers that Mom had thoughtfully provided and drank my milk. I stared at the chili for a while, and then I poured it back into the thermos bottle, sealed it up, and determined that I would never be subjected to this kind of humiliation again. For the rest of that school year, the chili remained entombed in that thermos. In my locker.

Up until the Christmas holidays, my Mom kept asking, "Where's that thermos bottle?" I kept saying that I didn't know, and after a while she stopped asking. When school let out in June, it was still there. I contemplated opening the thermos bottle in my health class, just to freak out the teacher, but I lacked the chutzpah. Instead, when I cleaned out my locker, I planted the dreaded chili, still safely sealed in its thermos bottle, safely and quietly in the garbage.

Undeterred by my own traumatic homemade lunch experience, I've adopted over the years a few hair-brained schemes of my own regarding the lunches that my boys cart off to school. There were the frozen pizza slices that apparently turned slimy when they thawed, and the labor-intensive nori-wrapped sushi rice with cucumber and smoked salmon. Once, I even packed my own idea of a great sack lunch—an apple, a chunk of cheese, and a handful of peanuts—but for some reason, the boys didn't go for it. "It's like you don't really care what we eat," one of them said. Worst of all were the handwritten love notes or words of encouragement my wife and I used to slip into the bags with their lunches. I know the guys must have found them irritating as hell.

The nutrition police will hate me for this, but I have discovered that the key to a successful homemade school lunch is to provide—along with a wholesome serving of whatever—a little junk food. And the best junk foods are the ones we make at home. A chocolate chip cookie is all well and good, but anyone can do that. How about a homemade sandwich cookie? Or homemade salted caramel corn? Now you're talking. Re-creating beloved processed foods at home may not be the healthiest thing for kids, but I do think making these things from scratch is better than purchasing the prefabricated versions. The flavors are intense and satisfying in a way that processed foods never are, and kids (and adults) are far less likely to eat more than a reasonable amount of a homemade treat. Plus, they communicate genuine caring to our children better than a potentially embarrassing handwritten note could.

FAUX-REOS

The National Biscuit Company (Nabisco) formed in 1898 and had its first major cookie hit with Barnum's Animal Crackers. But the animal-shaped cookies were eclipsed in 1912 when Nabisco introduced Oreos. The sandwich cookies struck a chord with the American public and quickly became America's favorite cookie. In this homemade, additive-free version, chocolate shortbread cookies are stacked with a simple vanilla frosting to make sumptuous snack cookies reminiscent of the familiar store-bought cookie. Don't be tempted to replace the palm kernel oil (organic shortening) with cheaper, typical hydrogenated oil.

For the cookies

1⅔ cups unbleached all-purpose flour

⅓ cup cocoa

1 teaspoon baking powder

½ teaspoon kosher salt

½ cup (1 stick) unsalted butter

½ cup organic palm kernel oil

⅔ cup sugar, preferably organic evaporated cane juice

1 egg

1 teaspoon vanilla extract

For the filling

¼ cup organic palm kernel oil

2 tablespoons water

1 teaspoon vanilla extract

2½ cups powdered sugar

◇ To make the cookies, whisk together the flour, cocoa, baking powder, and salt in a small mixing bowl. In a separate mixing bowl, whip the butter, palm kernel oil, and sugar with a hand mixer until light and fluffy. Mix in the egg and the vanilla extract, then stir in the flour mixture to form a dough. Divide the dough into 2 equal parts, and shape each piece of dough into a log about

6 inches long. Chill the logs in the refrigerator until they are firm enough to slice, about 1 hour.

◇ Preheat the oven to 350°F and line 2 baking sheets with parchment paper. Cut each log of chilled dough into 24 slices, each about ¼-inch thick, and arrange the slices 1 inch apart on the prepared cookie sheets. Bake the cookies until they are slightly puffed and uniformly browned on the surface, about 10 minutes. Completely cool on a rack.

◇ To make the filling, melt the palm kernel oil with the water in a small saucepan over medium heat. Stir in the vanilla, then stir in the powdered sugar. Continue stirring until the mixture is very smooth and creamy. Transfer the filling to a strong freezer-type ziplock storage bag and snip off one corner to make an impromptu piping bag.

◇ Finish the cookies by flipping half of the cookies upside down. Pipe a small amount (about 1 teaspoon) of the filling onto each overturned cookie and, before the filling sets, press another right-side-up cookie on top.

Makes 2 dozen sandwich cookies

REAL POPCORN

My wife and I raised our boys without a microwave oven; never had one, never wanted one. And I am perpetually baffled by the proliferation of microwavable popcorn. The stuff has become ubiquitous. Plain popping corn is worth seeking out, and actually popping the stuff in a heavy cast-iron or enameled iron kettle over a burner on the stove is serious fun. If you want to be sure that unpopped kernels don't get into the serving bowl, put the popped corn on a cooling rack over a sheet pan; the un-popped kernels will fall through, leaving the good stuff on top of the rack.

> ¼ cup corn oil
> ½ cup popcorn
> 6 tablespoons (¾ stick) unsalted butter (optional)
> 1 teaspoon sea salt (optional)

◇ Put the oil in a heavy cast-iron or enameled iron stockpot or Dutch oven over high heat. Have a large mixing bowl ready beside the stove.

◇ When the oil is very hot and just beginning to smoke, add the popcorn. Cover the pot, but leave the cover slightly ajar to allow steam to escape. Using pot holders, shake the pot gently from side to side or in a circular motion to keep the kernels inside the pan in constant motion. Continue shifting the pan as the kernels begin to pop. All the corn kernels will pop almost simultaneously and the pot may begin to overflow. If it does, pour off some of the popped corn and put the pot back on the burner for a moment or two until the popping sounds subside. Pour all the popped corn into the mixing bowl.

◇ If you want buttered popcorn, give the stockpot a rinse in cold water to cool it down, wipe it dry with a paper towel, and then put it back on the burner and melt the butter. (If you melt the butter in the pan without cooling it down first, it will burn.) Drizzle the melted butter over the popped corn and sprinkle with salt to taste.

Makes about 1 gallon, serving 4 to 6

SALTED CARAMEL POPCORN

All my efforts to make caramel corn were less than satisfactory until I found a recipe for Spicy Buttered Popcorn in Jennifer McLagan's wonderful book Fat. *That recipe relies on a stick of butter and a healthy dose of pureed chipotle peppers, and the results are great. But what really excited me about McLagan's recipe was the half teaspoon of baking soda added to the caramel coating just before it's tossed with the popcorn. That bit of culinary chemistry causes the caramel syrup to foam up so that it can be distributed evenly over the popped corn without clumping. Even though this recipe calls for completely different ingredients, it owes a lot to McLagan's innovation.*

½ teaspoon baking soda

⅓ cup plus 2 tablespoons water, divided

1 cup sugar

⅓ cup corn syrup

⅓ cup corn oil

2 tablespoons molasses

1 gallon popped popcorn

1 teaspoon fine sea salt

◇ Preheat the oven to 225°F and line a rimmed baking sheet with parchment paper.

◇ Dissolve the baking soda in 2 tablespoons of the water and set aside. Combine the sugar, corn syrup, corn oil, molasses, and the remaining ⅓ cup water in a very large Dutch oven or heavy saucepan. Stir the mixture over medium-high heat until the sugar melts and the mixture comes to a boil. Stop stirring and allow the mixture to boil until it reaches 250°F on a kitchen thermometer, about 5 minutes. Take the pan off the heat and stir in the dissolved baking soda.

◇ Immediately add the popcorn to the caramel mixture and stir with a heatproof silicone spatula or a wooden spoon until the popcorn is evenly coated. Spread the popcorn on the prepared baking sheet, sprinkle with the salt, and bake for 25 minutes, stirring 2 or 3 times. Cool to room temperature before serving. Store any leftovers in an airtight container.

Makes 1 gallon, serving 12

A TROUT-FISHING AMERICAN

"Oh, may I go a-wandering
Until the day I die
Oh, may I always laugh and sing
Beneath God's clear blue sky!"
—ANTONIA RIDGE

There is fried fish, and then there is fried brook trout from a mountain stream. My father-in-law always had a pretty good appetite and he was appreciative of my cooking, but he considered it "only fair" compared to anything he cooked himself over an open fire when he was in his beloved woods.

My own father is not what you'd call "outdoorsy." His idea of the great outdoors is more akin to a golf course than to a mountain trail. So when I fell in love with a girl from the Pacific Northwest, it took me a while to get used to her father's idea of the great outdoors. Born to a couple of pioneer types who opened the first bank in Seward, Alaska, before returning to Washington State in the 1920s, William Erich Lucas was a true outdoorsman. He lived to hike, camp, ski, and fish.

When I was still in my twenties and considered myself something of a hiker, I could never quite keep up with him on a mountain trail, even though he was already into his sixties. Erich never felt like he'd really gotten out of the house until he had trekked at least a mile or two away from the car, which he would leave along the side of one of the unmapped logging roads that meander into the foothills of the Cascade and Olympic Mountains. And his five daughters (my wife is his youngest) have all inherited, to some degree, his passions, especially the one for trout fishing.

"Some fathers worked," reported one of my sisters-in-law. "My father fished; fly-fished, that is. Not that he didn't work at fishing—he did—but for him, that kind of work was pure play." When I asked her to tell me about Erich's love of fly-fishing, she waxed poetic about her father's obsession. "It was the kind of play in which you got to hike up mountain streams, slip on mossy rocks, trip over rolling boulders, and otherwise splash about in search of the elusive brook trout that hid in shaded eddies, jumped impossible waterfalls, and fought the rushing torrents of water that swelled the streams in summer from the melting snow that came from somewhere higher up the hill. We kids got deposited beside the stream to loll in the meadow among the wildflowers until our father returned late in the afternoon laden with a creel full of beautifully colored fish, glassy-eyed, with their mouths still agape as if caught in surprise."

Over the years, Erich tried to teach me a little about trout fishing, but since I was the fifth in a long line of sons-in-law, and since I didn't seem to show much enthusiasm for the sport, he didn't push it. Instead, I persuaded him to let me gut the fish and fry them. He had always cleaned the fish himself, swiftly and with his back turned to the group, like a priest performing the old Latin Mass, so I could never see exactly how it was done. "Teach me how to clean a fish," I said. "You might not be here forever." Erich did, and it was from him that I learned about the thin coat of natural jelly, sparkling clear like the finest aspic, that coats a really fresh trout. And that since the scales are tiny and delicate, there is no need to scrape them, or the precious jelly, off the fish. Leaving the trout alone allows the cornmeal to cling to the fish without having to dip it in milk or egg or anything else that would gunk it up.

It was years before I realized what an honor it was that Erich allowed me to take over the trout cooking. Cooking the trout is, of course, one of the best parts of trout fishing, and Erich was as good at cooking trout as he was at catching it. He never went fishing without a portable frying pan, a flask of oil, and a pocket-size cache of cornmeal, salt, and pepper. (On overnight trips, he always brought along a little pancake mix and a small plastic bottle of maple syrup, too. He loved to have wild huckleberry pancakes ready for his daughters when they rose about an hour after he did.)

"One by one," recalls my sister-in-law, "he would add the fish to the frying pan while all of us kids lurked hungrily nearby, hoping he would choose us to give the first fish to. The smell of the oil and trout mingled with the scent of evergreen and heather. The fish were flipped expertly, at just the right moment, when the skin was crispy brown and the meat was tender, by leathery hands scarred with cuts and thickened with years of exposure to sun and rain, my father's hands that knew how to tie a fly and cast it out on the water with the grace of a dragonfly alighting on a lily pad."

When his trout-fishing days were behind him and Erich knew he was dying, his daughters took turns attending his bedside. Each one took a week to stay in the small apartment in Walla Walla where he and my mother-in-law, Patty, had chosen to finish out their days. They met at Whitman College there in the forties and thought that going back to Walla Walla made a kind of poetic bookend to their fifty-eight-year marriage. He asked one of the girls if he was dying. She said, "Yes, Dad, you are."

He thought about that for a second or two, took a breath, and then said, "Well, I guess we better have some ice cream."

After a while, he gave up eating altogether, and in the days that followed, he grew delirious. The girls offered him sips of water, but he shooed the glass away and said, "I'm drinking from those springs now." Eventually he slipped into a light coma, and we took turns sitting with him, reading to him, and talking among ourselves. I read aloud from one of his boyhood diaries to my son who is named for him. In the diary, he chronicled a trip to the National Boy Scout Jamboree in Washington, D.C., where President Roosevelt was going to light the bonfire. In every town where the train stopped for the night, Erich found a place to swim, and he logged his swims in his journal.

On the night he died, his wife, Patty, all his daughters, and a handful of his grandchildren were gathered around him. My mother-in-law had dementia and found the whole situation disconcerting.

"Someone should do something," she said. So I sat with her on a couch just outside the bedroom. I nodded and patted her hand and we listened to her daughters say their farewells to their father. Standing in a circle around his bed, my wife and her sisters sang all the songs they sang when they went hiking together with their dad—songs like "Funiculì Funiculà" and "The Happy Wanderer." The harmonies put their mother somewhat at ease. She began to tap her foot and nod her head agreeably from side to side.

Erich's breathing had slowed to long, loud, even inhales and exhales, deep and rhythmic, the very sound he made when he was hiking up a mountain trail, and I think we all imagined that he was leading the way, hiking ahead of us, hiking beside some stream we could never quite see. Then we heard the breathing stop, and one of the sisters said, "I think that's it."

Patty clutched my hand and looked at me with alarm. I said, "Do you want to go in there?"

"Yes!" she said, and so I helped her up and we made our way to the bedside. Patty bent down and kissed her husband and he gasped, took one last big breath, and let out a long, contented sigh. I don't think anyone's ever gone out of this world more peacefully.

PAN-FRIED TROUT

I have the greatest admiration for my trout-fishing father-in-law, but deep down, I am my own father's son, and the trout in my frying pan is likely to come from the Idaho Trout Company, a sustainable fish farming operation established in 1948. The technique I employ to fry it, though, is pure pioneer.

Four 6-ounce trout fillets with skin
2 teaspoons sea salt
1 teaspoon freshly ground black pepper
½ cup stone-ground cornmeal
Olive oil, for frying

◇ Preheat the oven to 250°F and line a baking sheet with a brown paper bag or a few paper towels. Season the trout fillets with the salt and pepper. Pour the cornmeal into a shallow bowl and dredge each trout fillet, coating both sides well; shake off the excess.

◇ Put enough olive oil in a cast-iron frying pan to make a ¼-inch layer, and heat over medium-high heat. When the oil is hot and begins to shimmer but is not yet smoking, fry 2 of the fillets until they are golden brown, then turn and cook the other side, about 5 minutes in all. Put the fried fillets on the prepared baking sheet and hold them in the warm oven while you fry the remaining fillets.

Makes 4 servings

HUCKLEBERRY OR
BLUEBERRY PANCAKES

Before we leave for a camping trip, I mix up the dry and wet ingredients for these pancakes separately; I store the wet ingredients in a jar in the cooler. Campfire-side, I stir them together just before I cook the pancakes. My father-in-law was one step ahead of me. He carried a little plastic bag full of his beloved Krusteaz-brand pancake mix, to which he added only water to make a batch of pancake batter. However you make the batter, just-picked wild huckleberries will make the pancakes better. At home, you might have to settle for domesticated blueberries.

1 ¼ cups unbleached all-purpose flour

1 heaping teaspoon baking powder

1 teaspoon baking soda

½ teaspoon kosher salt

1 egg

¼ cup sugar

¼ cup canola or corn oil

1 ¼ cups buttermilk

About 1 cup wild huckleberries (enough to cover 1 dozen pancakes) or fresh or frozen blueberries

◇ Preheat a griddle or a large cast-iron skillet over medium-high heat until a few drops of water bounce and sputter on the surface before evaporating.

◇ In a medium mixing bowl, whisk together the flour, baking powder, baking soda, and salt.

◇ In a small mixing bowl, whisk the egg with the sugar and, still whisking, stream in the oil. Whisk in the buttermilk, then stir the egg mixture all at once into the flour mixture, stirring just enough to bring the ingredients together. Do not overmix or the cakes will be tough.

◇ Rub a little butter or oil over the surface of the griddle with a paper towel. Spoon the batter onto the hot griddle and cover the surface of each cake with huckleberries or blueberries. When the pancakes are puffed and beginning to brown around the edges, after about 3 minutes, turn and cook until light golden brown and cooked through, about 2 more minutes.

Makes 12 pancakes

THE DON QUIXOTE
TOUR

*"Maybe the greatest madness is to see life as it is
rather than what it could be."*

—MIGUEL DE CERVANTES

Even though I go on and on about buying local and sup-
porting a community-based agriculture, I have certain
passions. I love coffee, for example, and as long as I can find
it and afford it, I have no intention of giving it up. I am pretty
fond of chocolate, too, and like coffee, cocoa doesn't grow
where I live. The same is true of olive oil, cinnamon, vanilla
beans, citrus fruits, and almonds. I am keenly aware that these
staple items in my kitchen come from far away, so I try to buy
them from sources that make sense. I like to imagine that by
buying these things, we improve the lives of others.

In his book *Terra Madre: Forging a New Global Network
of Sustainable Food Communities*, Carlo Petrini, founder and
president of Slow Food, describes how people's food choices

influence the lives of others, and not just those in our local foodsheds. He promotes "food communities" like farmers markets, but he goes beyond that, encouraging us to seek out and buy items that might otherwise disappear, taking a traditional way of life with them. People in Mauritania, for example, harvest a particular form of dried, salted mullet roe they call *bottarga*. If we support them by buying that product, we become what Petrini calls "coproducers." I don't often have the occasion to buy mullet roe, Mauritanian or otherwise, but I do know that if I buy coffee that's labeled "fair trade," "shade-grown," and "organic," I'm subsidizing programs that might help the people who harvest those coffee beans gain access to clean water and better schools. The "shade-grown" label assures me that the groves will provide a habitat for songbirds that spend half their time in my own hemisphere, and if the coffee is organic, the growers and their families will be exposed to fewer dangerous agricultural chemicals.

I can't say that I have any level of intimacy with the people who harvest my coffee, but I will say that I would like to meet them someday, and since the world seems to be getting smaller all the time, I just might. I had been using saffron for years, and it never occurred to me I might someday get to meet the people who harvested it on a regular basis, but a couple of years ago I did, when I accepted an invitation from the Trade Commission of Spain to tour the region of Castilla–La Mancha. I was in the home of Don Quixote, one of my all-time favorite fictional characters. For days, I would walk where Cervantes walked, visiting the windmills that he portrayed as giants in Quixote's mind and eating the foods that he ate.

The sun was blazing in the sky, and the dry soil crunched under our feet, but the air was decidedly cool. It was November, and I was standing in a field outside Madridejos, south of Toledo in Spain's Castilla–La Mancha region, home of the world's best saffron. There, under a clear blue sky, rows of small purple blossoms brightened the bare ground; no leaves were visible, just the petals of the autumn crocus, startlingly bright against the dull gray soil. This was *el azafrán*, "*el oro de La Mancha.*" The dried stigmas of those vibrant purple crocuses would be plucked, packaged, and eventually purchased by cooks around the world.

In culinary circles, saffron is known as the world's costliest spice. But locals, who use it in everything from rice dishes to tonics, savory sauces to ice cream and cakes, claim that the vibrant stamens and pistils of this autumn crocus are more than just a spice. They are medicinal, almost magical. Before we took to the fields, Antonio Garcia, president of the local saffron foundation, served the half dozen food writers I was traveling with a tea made of saffron and water. The tea was said to help one breathe easier, and hours later, inhaling the faint perfume wafting off a mounting pile of blossoms in the basket I carried, I did feel calmer, more focused, and generally more relaxed than I had in some time.

Gregoria Carrasco, a woman who sells the saffron she picks through the local saffron foundation, led us through the saffron fields and instructed us on how to harvest the blossoms. Legs spread wide to straddle the rows of delicate plants, we bent at the waist to pluck the flowers. A group of local pickers lined up side by side looked like a yoga class engaged in the wide-legged "standing forward bend," and I marveled at the agility of these people, most of them middle-aged folks like me. The work had to be done swiftly because the flowers bloom and die in the same day.

"All these people work at other jobs most of the year; none of them are used to bending like this," she said through a translator. "But everyone is happy because this is our favorite time of year." When she had explained all this, Carrasco sang a song about saffron. I couldn't understand all the words, but I got enough to know that it was a love song, sad and sweet, and when she reached the refrain, "how beautiful and precious are the fields covered in saffron," Carrasco dramatically swept her hand along the horizon so that we would take in the stark beauty all around us.

As soon as we had a basketful of blossoms, we were whisked off to a local household. There, a group of older women sat around a small kitchen table swiftly plucking the stigmas from the center of each blossom. And as the red-gold threads piled up, they were dried in a Chinese bamboo basket balanced over a space heater. I took a deep breath. The faint aroma that had wafted off the fresh flowers was considerably more intense as the filaments plucked from each blossom grew toasty over the space heater in this closed space. At one point, the homeowner lifted the basket and gave it a thrust so that the threads of saffron flipped in the air. "Smells good, doesn't it?" she asked in Spanish.

"They say that girls from La Mancha have no trouble finding a husband," said Carrasco, "because they smell like the rose of *azafrán*." At this, the women chuckled a little, but Carrasco took a more serious tone. "It's true that saffron is romantic," she said, "but it's a practical romance. You see my ring," she said, as she twisted her wedding band around her finger. "My husband bought this with money he earned picking saffron. And every year, with money from the saffron, we buy something we need for our home—the baby crib, new living room furniture, college tuition; and when I look at the things the saffron has bought us, I remember picking the blossoms, or plucking the threads like this in the kitchen. It's not an aphrodisiac, but it is romantic because everything that makes our lives a little better comes from the saffron, and it fills me with emotion."

On my trip, I learned that in recent decades, the cooperative that markets Spanish saffron is facing stiff competition from nefarious foreign growers who falsely claim that their saffron is from La Mancha. When I saw the difference between the real thing and the stuff grown in other regions, I gulped. I realized that I had been using falsely labeled, non-Spanish saffron for years. "How can they do that?" I wanted to know.

"You have to look for the '*denominación de origen*' label," I was told. "This year, we're working with a company to help us bypass the middleman and educate people about what a unique product this really is. A company called Costco is going to buy most of our saffron."

"Costco in Seattle?" I asked. As a Seattle chef, I had been teamed up with Costco executives any number of times at charity events and fundraisers; what's more, I frequently shop there. It was true—buyers from the company had been in town earlier that month and soon, the big-box company based in Seattle would be the world's single biggest importer of the world's best saffron.

When I got home, I spoke with Costco buyer Gary Kotzen. "We're really excited about this," he said, incredulous that I had been in one of the very fields where Costco's "next big thing" was being harvested. But I was equally incredulous. How could this truly artisanal specialty food find its way into my local warehouse store?

"It's what we're all about," claimed Kotzen, as if he were from marketing instead of purchasing. "We want the best of the best, and we want to offer it to our members without them having to pay the premium. We'll bring it in, package it ourselves, and offer it to our members at about a third or even a fifth of the cost of similar saffron. We did the same thing in 1997 with Tuscan olive oil. We did the same thing with handcrafted balsamic vinegar from Modena and most recently, with vanilla beans." Indeed, two glass test tubes, each containing five plump vanilla beans from Madagascar, were tucked away in my spice cupboard even as we spoke; I had, of course, purchased them at Costco.

"By mid-April, or perhaps early May, we'll have saffron from La Mancha in our stores, and it will be certified authentic with a D.O. label." So, for the rest of the winter, I lavished threads of red gold from La Mancha into my rice pilaf, stirred them into cream for a dessert sauce, and didn't worry about when the stuff in the little one-gram bottle I'd brought home from Spain would run out. I knew that in just a few weeks, I'd be harvesting next year's supply from the aisles of my local Costco store. I imagined myself rolling up to the checkout, humming a little tune: "How beautiful and precious are the fields covered in saffron."

Sadly, I never saw the saffron at Costco. Even though I shop there pretty often, it sold out before I ever got a chance to buy any. But oddly enough, saffron has been popping up closer to home. In Sequim, an Olympic Peninsula town relatively close to my home on Bainbridge Island, a man named

Jim Robinson is growing saffron crocuses commercially at his Phocas Farms. Of course I'm all for it, but no matter how close to home it's grown, it won't be any closer to my heart than the stuff that's picked by Gregoria Carrasco and her friends in La Mancha.

Cooks have been struggling with issues surrounding the provenance of their ingredients for centuries. Even before technological advances made it possible for people to transport fresh food from one continent to another, spices, oil, and wine were traded along with other luxury goods between far-flung populations. And while certain cooks embraced these delicacies, others dismissed them as frivolous. Today's homemakers are not the first to deal with some ambivalence about trying to eat local and still enjoy a cosmopolitan diet. For me, I try to ensure that the bulk of my diet—most of my grains, pulses, fruits, vegetables, and animal foods—are grown and harvested reasonably close to home, but I gladly embrace the little extras that come from afar and add so much to my daily life.

CHICKEN WITH SAFFRON RICE

Less complicated than a classic arroz con pollo, which employs short-grain rice like the kind used for making risotto and usually includes pork and beer along with the other ingredients, this dish is streamlined to highlight the flavor and aroma of the saffron.

¼ cup olive oil

4 boneless chicken thighs, preferably from free-range, organic chickens

1 tablespoon kosher salt

1 teaspoon freshly ground black pepper

½ medium onion, peeled and chopped into ½-inch pieces

1 medium red bell pepper, cored and cut into ½-inch pieces

4 cloves garlic, peeled and grated on a Microplane grater or finely chopped

1 cup long-grain white rice, such as jasmine or basmati

One 14.5-ounce can diced tomatoes, preferably organic

1 cup water

1 bay leaf

1 generous pinch (about 1 gram) saffron threads

◇ In a heavy saucepan or Dutch oven over medium-high heat, warm the olive oil; meanwhile, pat the chicken thighs dry with a paper towel and sprinkle them with the salt and pepper. Cook the thighs in the oil until they are lightly browned, turning them once to brown them evenly on both sides, about 5 minutes in all.

◇ Lift the chicken out of the pan and, in the oil left behind, sauté the onion, pepper, and garlic until the pepper is soft and the onion is beginning to brown, about 5 minutes. Stir in the rice, then pour in the tomatoes, water, bay leaf, and saffron threads and bring the liquid to a boil.

◇ Put the chicken pieces back in the pot, reduce the heat to low, and cover the pan securely. Simmer until the rice has absorbed the cooking liquid and the chicken is cooked through, about 35 minutes.

Makes 4 servings

MEDITERRANEAN MUSSELS WITH SAFFRON AND TOMATOES

Seafood guru Jon Rowley taught me to cook mussels in a dry pan before adding any liquid. Most recipes call for steaming mussels in wine or some other liquid, so the technique seems counterintuitive at first. But as the mussels sputter in the hot, dry pan, they release some of their juices on the hot metal and the juices caramelize into a tasty and evocative flavor base, which is eventually deglazed when liquid is added after the fact. Choose the largest Mediterranean mussels you can find for this dish. The aroma of saffron and mussels is evocative.

2 pounds mussels, cleaned and debearded
½ cup white wine
1 pound (about 2 large) ripe tomatoes, cut into wedges
3 or 4 cloves garlic, peeled and thinly sliced
1 generous pinch (about 1 gram) saffron threads
Crusty bread, for serving

◇ Heat a shallow pot or wok over high heat and add the mussels, tossing them in the dry pan until they spill enough of their juices to make a small puddle in the bottom of the pan, 3 to 5 minutes. Discard any mussels that do not open.

◇ Add the wine, tomatoes, garlic, and saffron. Cover the pan and allow the mussels to cook until they are cooked through, about 5 minutes longer. Serve the mussels in large, shallow bowls with their cooking liquid and some bread to soak up the juices.

Makes 4 appetizer servings or 2 entrée servings

NATURAL FOODS

"Avoid food products that carry health claims."
—MICHAEL POLLAN

Like most other Americans, I have been bombarded throughout my life with various messages, some of them more persuasive than others, about the advantages of eating whole, natural foods, as opposed to those that have been processed in a way that strips them of some of their essential nutrients. In tandem with this school of thought has been the notion that a truly healthy diet is a vegetarian one. Perhaps it goes without saying that I have been simultaneously bombarded with messages from natural foods skeptics and proponents of processed foods who claim that health food is rubbish.

The great Julia Child herself, who promoted healthy food in her own way by imploring cooks to use the freshest ingredients they could get their hands on and to make as many things from scratch as possible, was famously quoted as saying, "I just hate health food." She also took a strong stand against vegetarianism. "It's more fear of food," she said, "that whole thing that red meat is bad for you. And then there are people who don't eat meat because it's against their morals. Well, there's nothing you can do with people like that."

In the 1970s and early '80s, I didn't make much of a distinction between natural foods and vegetarian foods, and it seemed to me that no one else did, either. The behemoth meat and poultry industries seemed too daunting to naturalize, and most of us who considered ourselves proponents of natural foods were vegetarians. We had never heard of free-range, pasture-fed, or sustainably raised anything. It never occurred to us that meat could be organic or that eating animals could be part of a natural foods diet.

When I first encountered the natural foods movement and vegetarian cooking at that time, it was a full-fledged -ism, with zealous followers and a dogma that had roots spreading into every aspect of life. In my early teens, I embraced the movement with the passion of a convert. I started with giving up meat for Lent, to test the waters. By the time Easter rolled around, I had developed a certain abhorrence for meat; somehow, in order to overcome my initial cravings for it, perhaps, I had convinced myself that meat was not only unhealthy but wicked. I maintained this attitude for about a decade; then I gradually came to realize that refusing meat offered by well-meaning hosts was a greater moral offense than eating it.

At the alternative college I attended in Vermont, I lived in a vegetarian dorm where we cooked our own meals in a communal kitchen. As serious as Talmudic scholars discussing the laws of kashruth, my fellow vegetarian classmates and I wondered, "Should vegetarians wear leather shoes? Is it hypocritical to forgo meat and wear a leather belt?" And, with straight faces, we asked one another, "Does the gelatin in marshmallows make them bad?"

Most challenging of all, at least for me, was the question, "What do you do when you go home for the holidays and your mom has cooked a turkey?" The more zealous vegetarians gave little thought to their families' feelings; treating animals humanely and making decisions for the good of the planet were much more important to them. But I wasn't so sure. Food was the way my mother, her sisters, and her mother had always expressed their love for me, and if I refused their cooking, or anyone else's, I might be committing a moral crime as bad as, or even worse than, eating a dead animal.

Fortunately, my mother humored me with vegetarian stuffing at Thanksgiving and vegetarian versions of all her standard dishes the rest of the year. She made eggplant lasagna alongside her usual meat version, a smaller pot of potato curry beside her wonderful chicken curry, and vegetable quiche instead of her usual bacon dish. Two of my older brothers had gone through their own vegetarian phases, so by the time I gave up meat, she had become quite adept at keeping teenage vegetarians happy. We were all well versed in the complementary protein theory espoused by Frances Moore Lappé, whose *Diet for a Small Planet* was something like holy scripture for vegetarians. The creed went something like this: If only we'd feed grain and legumes to people instead of feeding those foods to animals, world hunger would end.

Combine any grain with any legume, and you have a complete set of the essential amino acids for human nutrition. Traditional diets like lentils and chapati, soy and rice, or pinto beans and corn—even peanut butter and Wonder bread—provide complete proteins from plant foods. Meat, if it was consumed at all in those diets, could be purely celebratory or sacramental and was not necessary. This was news to many Americans whose meat-centric diets were bolstered by the four food groups and, later, by the food pyramid (recently replaced by MyPlate) that helped the USDA promote the agricultural products of the American farmer, which included generous amounts of meat and dairy products.

But the job of the USDA has always been twofold. On the one hand, it has been about keeping us healthy; on the other hand, the organization has had an obligation to promote American products. By promoting the end products of an agricultural system that gives us a glut of corn and soy—as well as promoting the meat and dairy products that depend on government-subsidized corn and soy—the government is furthering a certain economic agenda. Sure, it sells that agenda with the notion that these animal foods are all about keeping us strong and healthy, but one certainly has to question the motives.

When I started becoming interested in the natural foods movement, the memories of the war in Vietnam and the protests against that war were still fresh in my mind. Less than a decade had passed, and juxtaposed against those violent memories played out on television—often during the dinner hour—the promptings of the government felt like the prodding of the beef handlers to move their steers to the slaughterhouse. It was as if the government wanted to keep us healthy so that we would be strong enough to go to war for our country. This thought might not have entered my mind consciously, but I did notice that most of the dietary guidelines issued by the U.S. government in the mid-twentieth century came in response to a population that failed, in large part, to measure up to physical requirements for the draft. Eating "right"—that is, eating a meat- and dairy-centric diet—was a patriotic duty.

So at the center of the natural foods movement was a nebulous antiwar sentiment and a not-so-vague antiestablishment message. The idea may have been communicated in an abstract and subliminal way, but somehow I gleaned that by saying no to meat, we were saying no to the whole military-industrial complex. We were standing on high, if somewhat shaky and ill-defined, moral ground. To a high school student, that antiestablishment attitude was almost as attractive as the idea that we vegetarians were saving the world, and I maintained that perspective as long as I stayed vegetarian.

My stance faltered when, on a series of occasions, I was invited to dinner by people I liked and admired, and I felt uneasy about asking them what would be served, especially because I knew it would probably be meat. In one instance, a friend convinced me that eating a share of the rooster he had killed and converted into a coq au vin would be good for me. I remember a particular time when, in my honor, a friend butchered a rabbit for dinner. It seemed unthinkable to say I couldn't eat it. On another occasion, some family friends had killed a number of quail to serve. The daughter had prepared devilled eggs from dozens of tiny quail eggs, and the matriarch of the family had made fried quail, along with beans, greens, corn bread, pickled okra pods, and sliced fresh tomatoes from her own backyard. I could have made a fine meal without the quail, but not to eat it would have insulted my hostess.

In his book *Eating Animals*, Jonathan Safran Foer's thoughtful treatise on how he became a vegetarian, he describes the challenge of maintaining a vegetarian diet in a culture where everyone else eats meat. We are social creatures; we want to be a part of the group. So at some point, re-embracing meat-eating was, for me, a way to accept my own culture as I had come to understand it. So it was partly peer pressure that drove me back to eating meat, but there was more to it than that. I was wrestling with genuine social and moral issues, and I was sorting them out as well as I knew how. By the mid-1980s, I was working full time as a line cook, and though I did not cook meat at home, I had relaxed out of my vegetarianism enough to eat meat when it was served as part of the family meal at work.

By that time, I had begun to learn about modern and traditional forms of animal husbandry that did not involve factory farming. And though I still thought of vegetarian and natural foods as somewhat separate from "regular" foods, those distinctions began to dissolve as my career progressed. In my first stints as a chef, fully in charge of what would go on the menu, I sought to balance ethically sourced local food with cuisine that had the broadest appeal. I wanted anyone who read my menu to immediately find something they wanted to eat, and I wanted anything they chose to be something I felt good about cooking. I was always very conscious about putting something on the menu for vegetarians, but more than that, I was putting food on the menu that was natural, prepared from scratch, and preferably organic. By the mid-1990s, when I was drafted to become the executive chef at Canlis Restaurant, which was and is one of Seattle's most important fine-dining establishments, I had earned a reputation as a chef who promoted the use of seasonal, regional ingredients, but I don't think anyone pigeon-holed me as a former vegetarian or thought me in any way antiestablishment.

I am still dedicated to using seasonal, regional ingredients. But more than that, I am a sentimental cook; I want everything I serve to be connected in some way to the story of the person who grew it, the animal that produced it, and the land from which it sprang. Whether I am serving Wagyu beef to a restaurant patron or mashed potatoes to my kids at home, I want to know and share something about how that food came to exist and how it connects us to the rest of the world. These days, it matters no more to me that the food is "natural" or certified organic than it does that it has a story.

Years after I left the restaurant, Mark Canlis was asked to provide a quote about what I did there, and he helped me see this about myself: "Atkinson has one hand on his All-Clad and one in the dirt," he told a reporter. "He's a storyteller, and he tells stories with his cooking."

Advances in animal husbandry have given me the option of eating meat that has a better story to tell than the factory farmed stuff I turned away from as a teenager. The steer in my freezer comes from a family that raises heirloom breeds of cattle on open grasslands in Eastern Washington. It never goes to a feeding operation. I frequently buy beef and pork from a place called Skagit River Ranch as well. The farmers there consider themselves grass farmers, and rather than add supplements to cattle feed, they add minerals and compost to the soil to keep their grass-fed cattle healthy. The cattle are never given antibiotics or steroids, and they are slaughtered in a mobile unit that comes directly to the farm, so they're never hauled off to a concentrated animal feeding operation (CAFO) or slaughterhouse. I feel good about eating that meat.

Of course, all the terms surrounding vegetarianism, organic standards, and natural foods are fraught with political and spiritual overtones, but for me, these terms are also tinged with nostalgia and positive associations with my own idealistic youth. So are the wonderful dishes that evoke the era when I was a teenage vegetarian. For some people, meat loaf conjures Mom's kitchen, but for me, so does a family supper of beans, greens, and corn bread, which is my family's go-to meal for "meatless Mondays" or any other night when we have time to soak the beans and slow-cook the greens. My family routinely eats vegetarian meals, not because we're avoiding meat, but because we really love these them and they are fun to cook.

WHITE BEANS

White beans such as great northern or cannellini are widely available and make an excellent old-fashioned pot of beans to be served as a simple family supper with slow-cooked greens and sweet corn bread.With a little grocery-store and Web sleuthing, some more interesting varieties of heirloom white beans can be found as well. Large, chestnut-textured corona beans; the extra-smooth heirloom cannellinis known as criollos; and the wonderful white lima beans known as butter beans are all delectable. These beans can all be prepared in the same way with a quick, preliminary soak, though larger and older beans will take somewhat longer to cook than smaller, fresher ones.

6 cups water

2 cups dried white beans

1 or 2 bay leaves

1 tablespoon salt

◇ In a large saucepan over high heat, bring the water to a boil. Add the beans, bay leaves, and salt. As soon as the water returns to a boil, turn off the heat. Cover the pan and leave undisturbed for 1 hour.

◇ Return the pot to high heat, bring the water back to a boil, and then reduce the heat to medium-low. Cook, covered, until the beans are tender but not falling apart, about 1½ to 2 hours, depending on the size and age of the beans. Check the beans from time to time as they cook, and if necessary, add just enough water to keep the beans barely covered. Serve the beans with greens and corn bread.

Makes 6 servings

SLOW-COOKED GREENS

My generation had a lot of laughs about how our parents' generation over-cooked their vegetables. But more and more, I am coming to realize that they were on to something. Certain vegetables—especially the tender tips and shoots like broccoli, asparagus, and peas—are essentially destroyed if you cook them for too long, but other vegetables, those that are mature and somewhat tough, can be infinitely better after a long simmer. And more than just the texture is improved: slow-cooked leafy greens like collards and kale take on new flavor dimensions when the cell walls break down and the harsh sulfide compounds contained within are given time to mellow and sweeten. Traditionally, these vegetables are cooked with smoked pork products, and I have been known to cook them in stock made from a ham bone, or to sauté a few strips of bacon in the pan before I throw in the greens, but I find that the real character of greens shines through best when they are simmered in a simple bath of sautéed onion and water.

> 2 bunches (about 2 pounds) dark, leafy greens, such as collard
>   greens or kale, thoroughly rinsed
> 4 tablespoons olive oil
> 1 medium onion, peeled and thinly sliced
> 2 teaspoons kosher salt
> 1 teaspoon freshly ground black pepper
> 1 cup water

◇ Hold each leafy green in one hand by the stalk, and with the other hand, strip the tender sides of the leaf away from the stalk. The stalk will generally break near the top where it becomes more tender; retain the leaves and the tender tops. Discard the tough central stems. Stack the leaves a few at a time on the cutting board, and cut them first lengthwise into 2-inch strips, and then across into 1-inch widths. Keep the greens near the stove.

◇ Heat the olive oil in a large saucepan over medium-high heat. Add the onion and cook, stirring occasionally, until the onion is soft and beginning to brown, about 5 minutes. Stir in the greens, salt, pepper, and water. Bring the mixture to a boil, then reduce the heat to medium-low. Allow the greens to cook, stirring occasionally, until they are very tender, 45 minutes to 1 hour. Check the greens frequently, and if necessary, add just enough water to keep them from drying out and sticking to the bottom of the pan.

Makes 6 servings

CAST-IRON SKILLET CORN BREAD

At some point, I came into one of those cast-iron corn bread pans that molds corn bread into the shape of little corn ears; it has become my favorite way to bake corn bread. If one of those pans is not available, the corn bread bakes up beautifully in a cast-iron skillet. The preheated cast-iron gives the corn bread a particularly nice crust. You can also bake the batter in a muffin tin. If you can find whole grain cornmeal, it has a more pronounced flavor and a more interesting texture than the typical refined stuff. But be sure it smells fresh, and store any unused cornmeal in the freezer; the bran in the whole grain contains oils that give the meal a shorter shelf life.

> 1 cup unbleached all-purpose flour
> 1 cup cornmeal, preferably whole grain
> 1 tablespoon baking powder
> 1 teaspoon kosher salt
> 1 large egg
> ⅓ cup sugar
> ⅓ cup corn or canola oil, plus additional for greasing the pan
> 1 cup milk

◇ Preheat the oven to 400°F. Place a 9-inch cast-iron skillet or a cast-iron corn ear mold in the oven. (If you opt to bake your corn bread in a muffin tin, there is no need to preheat it, but do oil the cups or line the them with paper liners.)

◇ In a large mixing bowl, whisk together the flour, cornmeal, baking powder, and salt.

◇ In a medium mixing bowl, whisk the egg with the sugar and oil until the mixture is perfectly smooth. Whisk in the milk. Add the egg mixture all at once to the cornmeal mixture, and stir just until the dry ingredients are moistened. Do not overmix (some lumps are OK).

◇ Remove the preheated skillet from the oven and grease with a little oil, about 2 tablespoons for the skillet pan or 1 teaspoon per corn ear mold. Be sure the surface is evenly coated. Pour the batter into the skillet, and bake until the bread is puffed in the center and golden brown, about 25 minutes for the skillet or 15 minutes for the mold or muffin pans.

Makes one 9-inch round loaf, 7 molded corn ears, or 12 muffins

SAVORY VEGETABLE QUICHE

Traditionally served at lunch or brunch, a vegetable quiche also makes a splendid casual supper with a glass of white wine and a tossed salad. One of the tricks to making a great crust for your quiche is to prebake the crust before you add the filling. To accomplish this without allowing the crust to buckle and rise up in the pan, line the empty pastry crust with parchment paper or foil, and fill it with pie weights for the initial baking. Specialty stores sell fancy ceramic or metal pie weights for this purpose, but dried beans or rice will work just as well, and they may be kept in a jar to be used again and again.

For the crust

1 cup unbleached all-purpose flour

½ teaspoon kosher salt

½ cup cold unsalted butter, cut into ½-inch bits

¼ cup ice-cold water

For the vegetable filling

½ pound broccoli florets

2 tablespoons unsalted butter

1 teaspoon finely grated garlic

1 teaspoon finely grated ginger

½ pound mushrooms, thinly sliced

1 cup (4 ounces) grated Gruyère or other Swiss-style cheese

For the custard

3 eggs

1 ½ cups half-and-half

½ teaspoon kosher salt

¼ teaspoon freshly ground black pepper

⅛ teaspoon ground nutmeg (optional)

◇ To make the crust, preheat the oven to 400°F. In a food processor or mixing bowl, combine the flour and salt. Add the butter and process or combine with a fork until uniformly crumbly. Transfer the mixture to a mixing bowl and add the water. Handling it as little as possible, press the mixture into a ball of dough then transfer the dough onto a floured surface. Roll the dough into a 12-inch circle. Transfer the rolled-out dough to a 10-inch tart pan and cover it with a piece of foil or parchment paper. Fill the lined tart with dried beans or rice and bake it for 12 minutes. Remove the lining and cool before filling.

◇ To prepare the filling, bring a large pot of salted water to a full, rolling boil. Cook the broccoli until it is bright green and barely tender, about 3 minutes. Drain the broccoli and spread it out on a tray or a baking sheet to cool. Melt the butter in a large sauté pan over medium-high heat until it foams; add the garlic and ginger and cook for just a few seconds before adding the sliced mushrooms. Cook the mushrooms until they release their water, and continue cooking until most of the water has cooked off, about 5 minutes.

◇ To make the custard, in a mixing bowl, beat the eggs. Whisk in the half-and-half, salt, pepper, and nutmeg, if desired.

◇ To assemble the quiche, layer the broccoli, mushrooms, and cheese in the prebaked crust. Pour the custard mixture over the filling and bake until the quiche is puffed in the center and barely set, about 30 minutes. Serve hot or warm.

Makes one 10-inch pie, serving 6

A BETTER BRAN MUFFIN

"The raisins were so plentiful and rare."
—CHARLES DICKENS

Developing a new formula for an old recipe can be an exercise in frustration, or it can be a pathway to new and sometimes unexpected delights. Not long ago, I determined to find a better way to make a bran muffin. I wanted an easy breakfast treat that would be healthy and ready to go on a busy work and school day. The trouble was that even the best recipes for bran muffins yield something that's only pretty good the day it's baked, and just barely edible the next day. And in spite of how streamlined one makes the process, there is nothing quick or easy about baking from scratch on a busy weekday morning. I wanted something I could bake ahead and look forward to.

Several attempts to solve the problem on my own led to some pretty firm conclusions: First, a little extra fat and sugar make for a better bran muffin. Second, I like molasses. And third, raisins are an important part of a good bran muffin, but when they're surrounded by cakelike crumbs, they're more distracting than comforting.

The real revelation, the key to the whole puzzle of how to make a better bran muffin, came from a recipe in Nancy Silverton's book *Pastries from the La Brea Bakery*. To make her bran muffins better than ordinary, Silverton simmers raisins in water then purees them in a food processor.

This step stopped me in my tracks. It reminded me of a recipe I developed years ago for an extra-chewy molasses cookie. That textural quality had proved somewhat elusive until I read the ingredients of a commercially made iced molasses cookie that included raisin puree. Raisin puree may not sound particularly thrilling in itself, but I'm here to tell you that in baked goods, especially baked goods containing molasses, it can make a world of difference. I had been trying to create the perfect molasses cookie for years when I stumbled upon that revelation.

My quest began with a childhood trip to Texas. My father was raised in the hill country of central Texas, and by the time I was born, his family was spread out between Houston, Longview, and Dallas. Once a year or so, my father would pile us all in the family station wagon and drive across Alabama, Mississippi, and Louisiana to his home turf, and we would drop in on all our Texas kin. On one trip, we went to see his grandmother; she was a tiny woman who must have been about ninety years old at the time. She lived with her daughter, my Great-Aunt Lois, in a white clapboard house in a town called La Marque in Galveston County, near the Gulf Coast. Because both women were getting on in years, they kept the house very warm, and because the heat came from a gas-burning furnace below the house, a metal grate in the center of the house pumped out a strange, toaster-like smell that comes back to me whenever I think of them. But I digress.

Suffice it to say that a homesick and baffled little boy was made to feel happy and at home when his great-aunt gave him a chewy molasses cookie, and when he grew up, he spent considerable effort trying to recapture that moment of cookie-induced bliss. The cookie Great-Aunt Lois gave me was store bought, and I tried a lot of brands of iced molasses cookies trying to find one as good as the one I had then. Somehow, I never found a cookie that tasted quite like that one. Raisin puree was the key that unlocked the puzzle, and as soon as I read Nancy Silverton's formula for bran muffins, I knew she was on to something.

If the raisin puree was a stroke of genius, other aspects of Silverton's recipe were daunting. Her formula included the tedious step of toasting the bran, and it omitted the molasses, an element I consider essential; what's more, the recipe made more batter than 12 muffin cups would hold. The cumbersome procedure and the finished product were not exactly what I was looking for. But, armed with the idea of pureed raisins, I was ready for another go.

ICED MOLASSES COOKIES

Cook the raisins, puree them with sugar, oil, and molasses, and you're on your way to a cookie that's likely to prompt nostalgic reveries of your own. A puree of raisins and an egg yolk in the dough make these molasses cookies extra chewy. A light icing made from the egg white makes the cookies extra special.

For the cookies

½ cup raisins

¼ cup water

½ cup canola or corn oil

1 cup brown sugar

½ cup light molasses

1 egg yolk

2 cups unbleached all-purpose flour

2 teaspoons baking soda

1 teaspoon ground ginger

½ teaspoon cinnamon

½ teaspoon allspice

½ teaspoon kosher salt

For the icing

1 egg white

1 cup powdered sugar

1 teaspoon vanilla extract

◇ Preheat the oven to 350°F and line 2 baking sheets with parchment paper.

◇ In a small saucepan over medium-high heat, combine the raisins and water. When the water begins to boil, reduce the heat to low and let the raisins simmer until they are plumped and soft, about 5 minutes. Transfer the raisins and their cooking liquid to the work bowl of a food processor and process until the mixture becomes a rough puree. With the motor running, stream in the canola oil, brown sugar, molasses, and egg yolk.

◇ In a separate medium bowl, whisk together the flour, baking soda, ginger, cinnamon, allspice, and salt. Add the flour mixture all at once to the raisin mixture and pulse the food processor on and off just until the mixture comes together to form a sticky dough. Do not overmix.

◇ On a lightly floured surface, divide the dough into 4 pieces and cut each piece of dough into 6 pieces, rolling the pieces quickly to form balls. Arrange the balls on the prepared baking sheets, allowing plenty of room for the cookies to spread. Bake for 5 minutes, then move the top tray to the bottom of the oven and the bottom tray to the top of the oven. Continue baking until the cookies are cracked and lightly browned, about 5 minutes more.

◇ While the cookies are baking, make the icing by whipping the egg white in a small mixing bowl until it holds soft peaks. Stir in the powdered sugar and vanilla. Transfer the icing to a small plastic sandwich bag and snip off one corner of the bag to make an impromptu pastry bag. When the cookies come out of the oven, drizzle the frosting over the tops of the cookies. Allow the cookies to cool to room temperature before removing them from the sheet pans.

Makes 24 cookies

MOLASSES AND RAISIN BRAN MUFFINS

Simmering the raisins in water, then pureeing them in the food processor provides a rich and satisfying foundation for these bran muffins, elevating them above the commonplace. They are crisp on the surface, light and sweet on the inside, almost like a fluffy, spice-free version of a molasses cookie. This is a breakfast bread that not only is fairly quick and easy, it also holds up for several days in the bread box. Plus, just one muffin will leave you satisfied until lunchtime.

1 cup raisins

1 cup water

½ cup canola or corn oil

½ cup sugar

½ cup light molasses

1 egg

1 cup unbleached all-purpose flour

2 teaspoons baking powder

½ teaspoon baking soda

1 teaspoon kosher salt

2 cups wheat bran

◇ Preheat the oven to 400°F. Put paper muffin liners in the cups of a 12-cup muffin tin. Lightly spray the papers with nonstick cooking spray or brush them with a light coat of canola oil.

◇ In a small saucepan over medium-high heat, combine the raisins and water. When the water begins to boil, reduce the heat to low and let the raisins simmer until they are plumped and soft, about 5 minutes. Transfer the raisins and their cooking liquid to the work bowl of a food processor and process until the mixture becomes a rough puree. With the motor running, stream in the canola oil, sugar, molasses, and egg.

◇ In a separate medium bowl, whisk together the flour, baking powder, baking soda, and salt, then stir in the wheat bran. Add the raisin mixture all at once to the dry mixture and stir just until the dry ingredients are moistened. Do not overmix.

◇ Distribute the batter evenly among the prepared muffin cups and bake until the muffins are browned on top and springy to the touch, about 20 minutes.

◇ Cool the muffins on a rack for at least 10 minutes before serving. Muffins will keep in an airtight container for up to 3 days.

Makes 12 muffins

ON BREEZE STREET

What are you makin', Son?" asked my mother, and her
tone was so purely inquisitive, so completely innocent,
that I had to smile. She sounded like a child. I could almost
hear myself asking her the same thing.

"What are you making, Mama?" I know I must have
surely asked a thousand times standing in that same kitchen
by the same round table where she was sitting now. I was
back in the house where I grew up, a house on Breeze Street
in Gulf Breeze, Florida. She should have known what I was
making. We had been talking about it all day.

"We're making gumbo, Mama." I already had some
chicken thighs simmering on the back of the stove, and the
meat and its broth would eventually be incorporated into the

stew. I was pouring oil and measuring flour into her heaviest pot to prepare the roux.

Mom swallowed and tried to look brave. "You'll have to tell me what to do," she said.

"I'm going to make the roux," I said, "and you can cut up some peppers and onions and celery." She rested both hands, palms down, on the table in front of her and sat up very straight. For just an instant I caught a glimpse of the woman she had been when she wore her hair in a bun behind her head and kept it dyed a dark brown, almost black. Now it was cut short and had gone from silvery gray to ghostly white. Her poise and confidence had given way long ago to a kind of fretful nervousness.

I unpacked the vegetables and got out a cutting board, the same one I remembered using when I was barely big enough to manage a knife. I decided against the big, stainless steel blade I would have used and chose a smaller knife with a thin, carbon steel blade and a wooden handle.

"You're going to let her use a knife?" asked my sister Annie, rolling her eyes and making an exaggerated *O* with her lips.

"Well," I said, "she let me use a knife when I didn't know what I was doing. And besides, it's all muscle memory. She can chop some vegetables."

Mom was watching us both, eyes moving from one to the other as if we were playing a very slow game of Ping-Pong. I gave her shoulders a little rub and said, "You'll be fine, Mama." I hated it when we started to talk about her like she wasn't there, even though in some sense, she wasn't.

"Mama hasn't really cooked anything in years," said my sister. She was pouring herself an iced tea.

Mom turned her hands palms up now and rolled her own eyes. "Who does she think cooks her supper every night?" she asked no one in particular.

"I don't know," I said to my mother. "Annie's been doing a lot of cooking these days." My sister was older than I was, well into her fifties, and for the last few years, she had been working double duty, cooking and cleaning for my mother and father even while she was holding down a full-time job as an office manager for a local orthopedic surgeon. When my father put out a call for help with Mom, my sister was the only one of the six children able to heed the call. Her own son was grown, and now she was living in my parents' old bedroom upstairs. They had moved into a main floor bedroom to keep Mom off the stairs.

"Y'all be careful," Annie said. Then she took her iced tea, sighed wearily, shaking her head as she headed off, wanting no part of the whole thing.

"How do you want these cut?" asked my mother, holding the knife in one hand and a green bell pepper in the other.

"Just the regular old way," I said. "Just like you showed me." I wasn't sure if a phrase like "half-inch dice" would mean anything to her.

As I started stirring flour and oil in a deep kettle at the stove, my mother set earnestly about the task of cutting up the peppers and onions and proved that my hunch had been right. Her hands remembered what to do. The peppers were reduced to small dice with the seeds and cores off to one side. The onion was stripped of its skin and chopped, too.

"How much of this celery are we going to need?" asked Mom, and for a moment, everything was so wonderfully normal that I could almost forget that she was fading away, that she couldn't sleep at night, wandering instead through her home of more than forty years, wondering where she was and what had happened to everyone.

She obsessed about my father and would start to panic if he was out of sight for more than a few minutes. Pop told me that there were times when she would get hysterical and demand that he take her home. She would claim that her mother needed her or that her daddy was dying and she had to get back there before it was too late. But for those moments while she chopped the vegetables and I stirred the roux, everything was as it had always been, and I held on to the illusion that it could be this way a little longer.

"You know what we should have with the gumbo?" she asked, suddenly inspired.

I knew what she was thinking, but I didn't know if she could verbalize it.

"What?" I asked.

Her face went blank.

"Waldorf salad?" I offered. It had been a generations-old tradition in our family to serve apple and celery salad whenever we served gumbo.

"Yeah!" she said, smiling broadly.

"Don't worry," I said, "I got some apples and pecans at the store, and I'm going to make some homemade mayonnaise."

When my father started to discuss having my mother installed in a nursing home, I resisted. But I live too far from home to be of much help, and the decision was really his to make. Back home in Washington, I had nightmares. In one dream, my mother was high in a black walnut tree at my grandmother's house, and I was on a ladder trying to coax her down. "How did you get up here?" I wanted to know. "I don't know," she said.

In a few short months, the next time I could get to Florida to visit, I would go to see my mother in a nursing home. She was eating canned cherries and artificial whipped cream from a Styrofoam box when I found her in the dining room.

"How did you find me?" she asked.

"I knew where to look," I said. "I knew you'd be at the table." She got the joke and laughed a little. She offered me some of her cherries and cream. At first I thought I would say no, but that would have been rude, so I took a bite.

"It's good," I said. "But I wish we could make some gumbo."

Later, I told her about the strange dream I had. "You were up in that black walnut tree in Grandma's yard, and I was trying to help you down."

She listened intently, nodded, and said, "I remember that."

"How are you doing here?" I asked.

"I'm scared," she said.

When I tucked her into bed for a nap, she persuaded me to climb onto the bed with her. "Just hold me a little while," she said. "I don't want to die," she whispered. "But sometimes I reach my hands up like this and I can almost feel my daddy's hands reaching for me. And I know he's there waiting for me." Then she said something that baffled me. "I know you're there, too," she said. "So I know it's going to be alright."

"You get some rest, Mama, and don't worry. I'll stay right here until you're asleep and I'll see you again real soon."

It was months before I could get back to Pensacola to see her, but when I returned, I brought my wife and sons with me. By this time, Mom was installed in a wheelchair and moving her was complicated. We lifted her into the rental car, put the wheelchair in the trunk, and brought her back to the family home, and there I cooked up another batch of gumbo.

CHICKEN AND OYSTER GUMBO

Okra came to the Gulf Coast with African slaves who developed the original gumbos. In several West African dialects, "gumbo" once meant okra. But in colonial Louisiana, soups were so often made with okra that gumbo came to mean almost any soup, with or without okra. (In winter, when okra was not available, sassafras, a seasoning borrowed from the local Choctaw people, was added to gumbo to give it its characteristic texture and to lend it more healing power.) Immigrants added their own spins across the years, and contemporary versions of the soup run the gamut from those with okra and seafood to soups with neither okra nor seafood. For my family, chicken and smoked oysters were the standard components. If fresh crabmeat was available, we always added some of that too.

For the chicken and broth

> 3 pounds bone-in chicken thighs
>
> 8 cups water
>
> 2 tablespoons kosher salt
>
> 2 bay leaves

For the roux

> ½ cup peanut or corn oil
>
> ½ cup unbleached all-purpose flour

For finishing the gumbo

> 1 medium onion, peeled and sliced
>
> 1 green bell pepper, cored and diced
>
> 2 stalks celery, diced
>
> 4 cloves garlic, peeled and finely chopped
>
> 2 teaspoons dried thyme leaves, divided
>
> 1 teaspoon freshly ground black pepper, divided
>
> ½ teaspoon cayenne pepper, divided
>
> 2 cups peeled, chopped tomatoes

4 cups sliced okra (fresh or frozen)

Two 3-ounce cans smoked oysters

8 ounces lump crabmeat (optional)

Cooked long-grain rice, as an accompaniment

◇ To cook the chicken and make the stock, combine the chicken thighs, water, salt, and bay leaves in a large pot. Cook over medium-high heat until the water begins to boil, then reduce the heat to low and simmer, covered, until the meat is very tender, about 1 hour. Lift the chicken thighs out of the simmering liquid with a slotted spoon and spread them out on a plate to cool. When the chicken is cool enough to handle, pull the meat off the bones and set it aside. Pile the bones and skin back into the broth. Allow the broth to simmer, uncovered, while you proceed.

◇ To make the roux, combine the oil and flour in a large soup pot with a heavy bottom over medium heat, stirring constantly with a wooden spoon until the roux is deep brown, about 20 minutes. Watch the roux closely to prevent burning. The darker one can get the roux without allowing it to burn at all is the test of a gumbo maker's skill. The key is to keep stirring, allowing a uniform deep brown to develop without ever allowing any of the flour to stick and blacken on the bottom of the pan. If any sticking and blackening does occur, carefully discard the roux by scraping it into a garbage can lined with several layers of brown paper, wash the pan, and begin again.

◇ Add the onion, bell pepper, and celery and cook until the vegetables are soft, 5 to 7 minutes. Stir in the garlic, 1 teaspoon of the thyme, ½ teaspoon of the black pepper, and ¼ teaspoon of the cayenne pepper. Immediately strain the chicken broth directly into the vegetable and roux mixture, stirring to prevent lumps from forming.

◇ Stir in the tomatoes, okra, and reserved chicken meat. When the soup is boiling once again, reduce the heat to low. Allow the gumbo to simmer for about 30 minutes.

◇ To finish the gumbo, stir in the smoked oysters, crabmeat, and remaining 1 teaspoon thyme, ½ teaspoon black pepper, and ¼ teaspoon cayenne pepper. Cook until the seafood is heated through, about 10 minutes. Serve with the rice.

Makes 12 servings

WALDORF SALAD

It's no secret that, like mustaches, recipes go in and out of fashion. But some recipes never really go away. Waldorf salad was introduced at the Waldorf Astoria Hotel in 1896, and it has been pretty much in vogue ever since. My grandfather, who managed a grand old hotel in my hometown, did an internship at the Waldorf Astoria in the 1920s and brought the recipe for the salad home with him. My family has claimed a special connection to the salad ever since. I like it best the way my mother made it, with equal parts tart-sweet Winesap apples, celery, and toasted pecans. If red-veined Winesaps are not available, use another tart, crisp apple.

½ cup pecans

2 pounds (about 4 medium) tart, crisp apples

1 tablespoon freshly squeezed lemon juice

1 tablespoon sugar

4 or 5 stalks celery from near the center of the head

⅓ cup Homemade Mayonnaise (page 123), or a high-quality store-bought mayonnaise

1 teaspoon kosher salt

½ teaspoon freshly ground black pepper

◇ Preheat the oven to 300°F. Toast the pecans until they are very fragrant, about 7 minutes. Allow the pecans to cool while you prepare the salad.

◇ Peel, core, and cut the apples into ½-inch dice. Toss them immediately in a salad bowl with the lemon juice and sugar.

◇ Cut the celery across the stalks into ¼-inch slices. Include any leaves that are attached.

◇ Toss the celery with the apples, then fold in the mayonnaise and the toasted pecans. Season with the salt and pepper.

Makes 6 servings

IN THE VIEUX CARRÉ

"The river rose all day
The river rose all night
Some people got lost in the flood
Some people got away alright."
—RANDY NEWMAN

Three years after Hurricane Katrina devastated New Orleans, the city was still trying to pull itself back together. I had some time off, so I signed on to cook for a group of high school students from Bainbridge Island who were going there to work with the relief agency Habitat for Humanity. We camped out at a church in one of the less affected neighborhoods, and there, I set about trying to re-create all the dishes I had loved when I was growing up on the Gulf Coast. I figured that as long as the young people were in the area, they might as well get a taste of the local food.

Every day for a week, the students and the other adult volunteers would take off for the building site. I would head out with them and spend the morning working beside them.

After we enjoyed a sack lunch I'd packed for us that morning, I would head out to shop and cook for the rest of the afternoon. I sought out the farmers market in the parking lot behind Tulane University, became something of a regular at the Rouses supermarket on Tchoupitoulas Street, and indulged in a little time alone by enjoying a coffee and newspaper almost every afternoon at a Community Coffee store—the New Orleans version of Starbucks—on Magazine Street. (I justified the leisure time by working hard cooking and cleaning while the rest of the group relaxed after returning from the building site.)

In the past, I had always visited New Orleans as a tourist, and my trips to the city were largely confined to the Vieux Carré, the part of town that people call the French Quarter. My parents often took us there when my brothers and sisters and I were growing up, and when I brought my own kids to the Gulf Coast to visit my family, we often spent a day or two in New Orleans for fun. But this time was different. I had always felt a certain nostalgia for the place, but spending those afternoons alone in the Crescent City made me feel connected to the place in a whole new way. And one afternoon, sipping my coffee and contemplating the afternoon's cooking agenda, I flashed back to something my friend Ruth Beebe Hill said when the two of us were reminiscing about good times we had both had there.

"I never miss New Orleans more," she said, "than when I'm sitting right in the heart of it." With her shock of red hair, seated regally in one of her beloved straight-backed chairs, Hill was sipping a Sazerac, the famous cocktail of New Orleans, and holding court in her living room.

Most people who know of Hill know her as the author of *Hanta Yo*, a controversial novel about the Plains Indians that she researched for thirty years, going so far as to learn the archaic language of the Lakota Sioux. She translated key passages and phrases of the novel into that language, then translated them back into English to capture the rhythm of the original Lakota. Criticism of her work stemmed from her depiction of the Sioux as radical individualists, a characterization that probably had more to do with Hill's fascination with her friend and mentor Ayn Rand than it did with the Lakota.

Born and raised in Cleveland, Ohio, she was a graduate of Ole Miss and a student of the great William Faulkner, and she'd always had a soft spot for the Deep South. During the early years of her marriage, in the mid-twentieth century, Hill spent a couple of decades in the Crescent City; she celebrated its distinctive Creole culture for the rest of her life. When I met Hill, she was in her seventies, living on San Juan Island and working as a freelance editor. I was working as a chef at her favorite restaurant on the island, and she used to hire me every year to cook for a Mardi Gras party at her house. Over a period of a decade or so, we became close friends, and I developed a habit of thinking about what to cook when Fat Tuesday rolled around.

"I know you love New Orleans, too," she once said to me, "and I want to know what you think of these people who say the city has lost its way." This was years before Katrina, and Ruth had taken it as an affront when one of her friends said the city was going downhill.

"It doesn't matter what people say," I assured her, jumping to the Big Easy's defense. "New Orleans can hold its own. It's a world unto itself." The city's unique cultural heritage had always impressed me as something beyond criticism. Its architecture, its cuisine, the propensity of its citizens to stay put for a lifetime, never venturing too far from their own neighborhoods, are characteristics that have always struck me as endearing.

"It's so easy to imagine being there," I said. "I can picture Jackson Square and the St. Louis Cathedral as if I had been there yesterday. And I can never forget the sights and sounds of Café Du Monde or the taste of those amazing beignets." Beignets, puffy square doughnuts, three to a plate, buried in a pile of powdered sugar, are the only food item on the menu at that café.

"Stop it," she said. "You're making me homesick."

But I couldn't stop. "If we were there right now," I said, "I would walk right past Café Du Monde and the old farmers market, down to Central Grocery, and buy us one of those muffuletta sandwiches." Made up of stacks of provolone cheese and salami layered between slabs of bread that have been smeared with a chopped olive salad, the muffuletta is one of New Orleans's most guarded and cherished culinary delights, ranking right up there with oysters Rockefeller and Creole gumbo.

That's when Ruth said that she missed New Orleans most of all when she was there. "It's a nostalgic place," she said. "But let's talk about something else." She was a pragmatic woman, never one to dwell on the past or what couldn't be achieved in the present. As I remembered all this, sitting there on the sidewalk outside the coffee shop, I suddenly felt guilty that I had dawdled too long while the others were working. I brushed off the wave of nostalgia and scrambled to get back to the church where we were camping out so I could start on dinner for the crew.

NEW ORLEANS–STYLE BEIGNETS

Café Du Monde, a coffee stand at one end of the French Market, has been serving hot beignets and café au lait twenty-four hours a day, seven days a week, since the place opened in the early 1860s. "Beignet" is a French word for fritter, and recipes for fritters in France are myriad; they can be almost anything fried. But in New Orleans, they can be only one thing: puffy, deep-fried squares of airy dough under a mountain of powdered sugar. Recipes for reproducing these things at home abound, but this one produces the real deal. When I was in my twenties, I turned in a stint as a brunch cook at a place where I had to make these doughnuts by the hundreds and I learned a trick or two. Southern flour is softer than most all-purpose flour, so if you can't by flour from the Deep South, like White Lily or Martha Washington brands, opt for cake flour. You can even omit the baking powder, baking soda, and salt from my recipe and use self-rising flour, but it has a little more leavening than you want. Don't use yeast to leaven the dough. Don't use eggs. Do use buttermilk.

    Corn or canola oil, for deep-frying

    2 cups soft white flour

    2 tablespoons sugar

    1 teaspoon baking powder

    1 teaspoon baking soda

    1 teaspoon salt

    1 cup buttermilk

    4 heaping tablespoons powdered sugar, for sprinkling

◊ Preheat the oven to 200°F. Line a baking sheet with a brown paper bag and put it in the oven.

◊ Preheat a deep fryer to 365°F. If no deep fryer is available, pre-heat at least 2 inches of corn oil in a deep, heavy stockpot over medium-high heat until a candy thermometer registers 365°F, or until a cube of bread dropped into the oil rises immediately to the surface and becomes golden brown in about 1 minute.

◇ In a large bowl, whisk together the flour, sugar, baking powder, baking soda, and salt. Add the buttermilk all at once to the flour mixture and stir just until the mixture comes together to form a soft dough.

◇ On a well-floured board, fold the dough over itself 1 or 2 times to firm it up, but don't knead it in earnest or the doughnuts will be tough. Roll the dough into a rectangle about 10 inches wide and 12 inches long, sprinkling with flour as needed to keep the dough from sticking. With a pizza cutter, cut the rectangle into 3 rows of 4 squares each.

◇ Lower the doughnuts, one at a time, slowly into the oil, frying no more than 3 doughnuts at a time (crowding the oil prevents the doughnuts from cooking properly). Fry until the doughnuts puff up and rise to the surface and the underside is golden brown, then turn them once. They should be puffed and golden brown on both sides.

◇ Lift the doughnuts out of the oil with a slotted spoon and drain them on the prepared baking sheet. Keep the doughnuts warm while you prepare succeeding batches. At serving time, sprinkle each serving of 3 doughnuts with 1 generous tablespoon of powdered sugar.

Makes 1 dozen beignets

MUFFULETTA SANDWICHES

Wherever you are, it's easy enough to evoke old New Orleans if you assemble a sandwich made with olives, salami, and provolone cheese. Named for the round Italian olive oil bread on which it was made, the sandwich originated in the Vieux Carré at Central Grocery in the early years of the twentieth century to satisfy the Sicilian farmers who sold their produce at the farmers market across the street. Today, the sandwich has become a mainstay of New Orleans groceries and sandwich shops. It sometimes includes mortadella and capicola as well as salami; it always includes the chopped olive salad that has become synonymous with its name. Load up on green olives stuffed with pimientos, and giardiniera, *an Italian relish of marinated vegetables readily found in American groceries. Or put together your own custom mixture of olives, peppers, and pickled vegetables sold at the olive bars of modern grocery stores. If you follow the formula below, you'll have about twice as much of the olive salad as you need for the sandwiches, but the extra salad keeps, covered and refrigerated, for several weeks.*

For the olive salad

One 16-ounce jar pimiento-stuffed green olives, drained
   (about 2 cups)
One 16-ounce jar giardiniera (mixed Italian pickle), drained
   (about 2 cups)
¼ red onion, peeled and chopped
¼ cup extra-virgin olive oil
4 cloves garlic, peeled and minced
1 teaspoon dried oregano
1 teaspoon dried basil

For the sandwiches

4 soft kaiser rolls, or a 1-pound loaf of focaccia cut into 4 pieces
8 ounces salami, or a combination of salami and mortadella
Four 1-ounce slices provolone cheese

◇ To make the olive salad, combine the olives, giardiniera, onion, olive oil, garlic, and herbs in a food processor and pulse the motor on and off until the mixture is roughly chopped. Do not overprocess the mixture; the olives should not become a puree.

◇ Split the rolls or focaccia pieces in half and distribute half of the olive salad over 4 of the bread halves. Layer the salami and provolone on top of the olive spread and top with the other half of the bread. The sandwich may be eaten at once, or better still, wrapped in paper and held at room temperature for 30 minutes to allow the oil to soak into the bread and the ingredients to come to room temperature.

Makes 4 generous sandwiches

RED BEANS AND RICE

In New Orleans, and all over the Gulf Coast, for that matter, Monday used to be wash day. And since laundry in the days before machines was all consuming, preparing the meal of the day had to be pretty much a hands-free affair. According to tradition, a pot of red beans was the standard fare at every Creole house on Mondays. Another tradition was a Sunday ham, so most versions of red beans and rice include a ham bone or some cut-up ham in the pot. But the ham is superfluous. Beans and rice make a complete protein, and the Creole trinity of onions, celery, and bell peppers, with the traditional seasonings of garlic, thyme, and cayenne pepper, provide plenty of flavor. In a weird bit of serendipity, when you leave out the pork, the dish is almost identical to a red bean dish from India called "rajma," a red bean curry also served with rice; I like to play up the Asian connection by serving the beans with jasmine or basmati rice.

For the beans

6 cups water

1 or 2 bay leaves

1 tablespoon kosher salt

2 cups dried kidney beans

For the sauté

1/4 cup olive oil

1 medium onion, peeled and cut into 1/2-inch dice

4 stalks celery, cut into 1/2-inch dice

1 green bell pepper, cored and cut into 1/2-inch dice

4 cloves garlic, peeled and finely chopped

1 teaspoon dried thyme

1/2 teaspoon cayenne pepper

For the rice

3 cups water

2 teaspoons kosher salt

2 tablespoons unsalted butter

2 cups long-grain rice, such as basmati or jasmine

◇ To prepare the beans, in a large kettle over high heat, bring the water, bay leaves, and salt to a boil. Add the beans and as soon as the water returns to a boil, turn off the heat. Cover the pan and leave undisturbed for 1 hour.

◇ When the hour has passed, turn the burner on high and bring the beans to a boil again; reduce the heat to low and cook, removing the cover to stir occasionally. When you open the pan to stir the beans, check the water level and if necessary, add just enough water to keep the beans barely covered. Continue cooking until the beans are just tender, 1½ to 2 hours.

◇ When the beans are fork tender, prepare the sautéed vegetables. In a sauté pan over medium-high heat, warm the olive oil and cook the onion, celery, and bell pepper until the vegetables are soft and fragrant and the onion is beginning to brown, about 5 minutes. Stir in the garlic, thyme, and cayenne and cook until fragrant, about 1 minute more. Stir the vegetables into the beans, cover the pot, and cook for 30 minutes, or until the vegetables are very tender and the beans are beginning to fall apart.

◇ While the beans are undergoing their final simmer with the vegetables, prepare the rice. In a medium saucepan over high heat, bring the water, salt, and butter to a boil. Stir in the rice, reduce the heat to low, cover the pan, and allow the rice to cook, undisturbed, for 20 minutes. Remove the lid, give the rice a stir, and then return the lid and allow the rice to rest for 5 minutes before serving it with the beans.

Makes 6 servings

MY OLD KENTUCKY HOME

"Life is much too short for some folks
For other folks it just drags on
Some folks like the taste of smoky whiskey
Others figure tea is too strong."
—JESSE WINCHESTER

The winter solstice in these northern latitudes finds most of us rising before the sun and going to bed long after it's set. It would seem that what we need is light and warmth, but what we seem to crave is food—lots of dense, rich, calorie-laden food—and drink. And I have a theory about that: food and alcohol are essentially concentrated sunlight.

Think about it. Plants convert solar energy into carbohydrates. We eat those plants. Animals eat those plants, too, and convert the energy into more concentrated forms like fat and protein. We eat those animals. Under special circumstances, microscopic yeast can concentrate carbohydrates into energy-rich alcohol in the form of beer and wine, and when it's distilled, the energy is even more concentrated. A single gram of protein or carbohydrate provides four calories, but a gram of alcohol provides seven calories and a gram of fat provides nine calories.

Of all American foods, corn strikes me as the best illustration of captured, edible sunlight. Golden as the sun itself and studded with fat kernels fairly bursting with energy in the form of long carbohydrate chains, American corn was grown almost to the point of excess by the first European settlers who moved into the wild lands beyond the first colonies. When the states were first united, the federal government offered settlers land for free if they would clear the land and grow corn on it, so people did precisely that. To get added value from their corn in the marketplace, they fed the corn to pigs and transformed the pigs' flesh into bacon and hams. Other settlers fed their corn to yeast that converted it into alcohol; then they cooked that alcohol off its watery mash and saved the concentrated stuff in barrels. Folks are doing the same thing today, albeit on an industrial scale.

Whiskey and pork are more valuable commodities than corn in its raw form. This really hit home when I was touring Bourbon County outside of Louisville, Kentucky. Inside the "ricks"—warehouses where barrels of corn liquor are aged in row upon row of handcrafted, specially prepared oak barrels—it occurred to me that here was America's signature method of capturing sunlight.

In order to be labeled "bourbon" whiskey, a distilled spirit must be derived from grains, at least 51 percent corn. The spirits must be distilled to no more than 160 proof, aged in new oak barrels that have been charred on the inside, and finished with nothing other than water. In Bourbon County, the local water supply is naturally filtered through mellowing limestone, which removes every trace of iron, the nemesis of good whiskey. Whiskey may be legally labeled as bourbon wherever these requirements are met, but the qualifications are so readily and organically met in Bourbon County that making the stuff anywhere else hardly makes sense.

Full disclosure: I accepted an invitation from the Louisville Convention and Visitors Bureau, which serves as a sort of public relations firm for the city and, to some degree, the entire state of Kentucky. I agreed to explore their famous Whiskey Trail, and I visited distilleries by day and bars that transformed the product of those distilleries into classic cocktails by night. I met a man named Matt Jamie who makes soy sauce using local, organic soybeans and then ages it in used whiskey barrels under the brand name Bourbon Barrel Foods. While I was visiting his "factory," he received a water delivery from one of the local natural springs that also provides water for one of the distilleries I had visited earlier in the week. Between distillery tours, I stopped by Federal Hill, a plantation that's now a Kentucky state park and is said to be the place that inspired Stephen Foster's ballad "My Old Kentucky Home." I also toured the Louisville Stoneware factory, which was founded in 1815 and still produces wonderful handcrafted pots and dishes from local clay.

"We sold a lot of these large clay jars during Prohibition," said the man who was conducting an impromptu tour. "Folks said they needed the big jars for making sauerkraut," he added with a wink. Presumably the crocks were being used to ferment mash that would then be distilled into illegal hooch, moonshine, or, as the Kentuckians call it, white dog.

Gradually, over the course of a few slightly inebriated days, I came to fall completely in love with central Kentucky, and in that state of enamored bliss, I had what could only be called an epiphany. Here was the very essence of sunlight captured in a unique and very human way. We were standing in the distiller's workshop at Buffalo Trace Distillery, and warm September sunlight poured in through tall windows as a young distiller drew off some clear white dog at about 135 proof—pure, unaged, undiluted spirits derived from natural grains. I was spellbound.

"Corn converts the sunlight into sugar, and we convert the sugar into spirits," the distiller explained. "We water this down to 100 proof and put it into charred oak barrels to age." Even though the pure spirits were virtually undrinkable, the clear, burning essence of whiskey did indeed possess the quality of sunlight. It was clear, bright, and burning hot, and smelled—underneath its ethanol cloud—of fresh baked bread, of dry grass, of clean sheets dried on a clothes line on a bright sunny day. I likened it to sunlight concentrated through a magnifying glass. "That's right," she said, "you don't want to take it straight, but cool it off with a little ice and you'll be fine."

Ever since I returned to my home in Washington, I have carried a little torch for Kentucky, and come the dark days of winter, I set it blazing, uncorking a little of that concentrated sunshine known as Kentucky bourbon.

A NEW OLD-FASHIONED COCKTAIL

The old-fashioned is a classic cocktail in which simple syrup and bitters establish a foundation for what is more or less an all-whiskey drink garnished with muddled orange and a cherry. Even as early as the turn of the last century, variations abounded. Sometimes, for example, to enhance the presence of the orange, the standard aromatic bitters were replaced with orange bitters; or curaçao, an orange-flavored liqueur, was used in place of simple syrup. In this version, orange bitters and maraschino liqueur (I prefer Luxardo brand) do the job. In my home bar, Bing cherries steeped in maraschino liqueur stand in for the familiar maraschino cherries. But if you don't happen to have any of those on hand, pick up a bag of frozen maraschinos from your local grocery store.

I ounce maraschino liqueur, such as Luxardo brand

2 generous dashes orange or angostura bitters

3 ounces bourbon

I ounce soda water

2 orange slices

2 frozen Bing cherries

◇ Fill 2 highball glasses with ice cubes and keep them close at hand.

◇ Put the maraschino liqueur, bitters, and bourbon in a shaker and fill the shaker with ice cubes. Splash with the soda water. Cover the shaker and give it 5 or 6 firm shakes.

◇ Strain the drinks into the prepared glasses and top each drink with a slice of orange and a cherry.

Makes 2 drinks

OVEN-BARBECUED PORK WITH BOURBON SAUCE

Pork barbecue is something of an art in the American Deep South, and I am a bit reluctant to admit that I make an imitation version of the stuff without a smoker or a pit. I took a cue from Hawaiian cooks, who are also famous for barbecued pork. There, instead of digging the traditional pit-oven, or imu, *people routinely prepare kalua pig or barbecued pork by slow-roasting it in the oven with liquid smoke. I tweaked the Hawaiian method by adding a little Kentucky whiskey, which seems to conjure the spirit of the place, wherever it's poured.*

For the pork

¼ cup corn oil or lard

One 6-pound boneless natural pork shoulder

3 tablespoons kosher salt

¾ cup water

¼ cup bourbon

I teaspoon whole black peppercorns

¼ cup liquid smoke

For the barbecue sauce

¼ cup corn oil or lard

½ medium onion, peeled and cut into ½-inch dice

2 cloves garlic, peeled and finely chopped

¼ cup bourbon

I cup ketchup

½ cup brown sugar

¼ cup cider vinegar

I tablespoon liquid smoke

I teaspoon kosher salt

½ teaspoon freshly ground black pepper

◇ To roast the pork, preheat the oven to 300°F. In a Dutch oven or a covered casserole that can go from stovetop to oven, warm the oil over medium-high heat. Sprinkle the pork with the salt and cook it in the hot oil, turning it once, until it is browned on each side, about 10 minutes total. Pour in the water and bourbon then add the black peppercorns and the liquid smoke.

◇ Cover the pot tightly and bake the pork until it is very tender and shreds easily, about 3½ hours. If you are not serving the pork immediately, decrease the oven temperature to 200°F, leaving the door cracked open to cool the oven down more quickly. Remove the pork from the pan, shred it with your fingers or with a fork, and set it aside. Strain the liquid left in the pan, discarding the solids and returning the liquid to the pot. Return the pork to the pot with the strained liquid. The shredded pork may be kept in the warm oven, covered, for up to an hour.

◇ To make the sauce, heat the oil in a deep saucepan over medium-high heat and add the onion and garlic. Cook until the onion is tender and beginning to brown, about 5 minutes. Add the bourbon and carefully tilt the pan toward the flame or hold a long match to the edge of the liquid to coax it to light. Swirl the pan until the flames subside. Stir in the ketchup, brown sugar, vinegar, liquid smoke, salt, and pepper. Reduce the heat to low and simmer the sauce until it thickens slightly and the flavors mingle, about 15 minutes. The sauce may be made ahead and held at room temperature for 2 hours, or covered and refrigerated almost indefinitely.

◇ Serve the pork with coleslaw as an entrée, or use it as a sandwich filling. Pass the sauce separately.

Makes 12 servings

KENTUCKY BOURBON CHOCOLATE WALNUT PIE

Most Kentucky bourbon distilleries wrap up their tours by offering guests a piece of chocolate filled with a bourbon-spiked fondant. So when I came home from Kentucky, I was determined to put whiskey and chocolate together into a scrumptious dessert that would chase away any trace of the winter blahs. I turned to a barely remembered formula my mother used for chocolate walnut pie and spiked it liberally with bourbon.

For the crust

    1 cup unbleached all-purpose flour
    1 tablespoon granulated sugar
    ½ teaspoon table salt
    ½ cup (1 stick) unsalted butter, chilled and cut into ½-inch bits
    3 tablespoons ice-cold water

For the filling

    2 cups shelled walnuts
    ⅓ cup walnut oil
    6 ounces bittersweet chocolate, cut into ½-inch bits
    ¾ cup brown sugar
    ¾ cup corn syrup
    3 large eggs
    3 tablespoons bourbon
    1 teaspoon vanilla extract
    ½ teaspoon table salt
    Lightly sweetened whipped cream, for garnish (optional)

◇ To make the pie crust, combine the flour, granulated sugar, and salt in a food processor fitted with a steel blade. Pulse in the butter, turning the motor on and off until the mixture resembles coarse crumbs, then transfer the mixture to a medium mixing bowl. Splash the cold water over the flour and butter mixture and mix with your fingertips or a rubber spatula until the mixture comes together to form a shaggy mass of dough. Don't overwork the dough or try to make it smooth.

◇ Transfer the dough to a well-floured work surface and roll it into a 12-inch circle. Transfer the rolled-out dough to a 9-inch glass pie pan. Trim the edges of the dough to make a ½-inch overhang, then tuck the overhanging dough under so that the folded edge is flush with the rim of the pan. Flute the edges, if desired, to create a decorative border. Transfer the pie crust to the refrigerator and chill for at least 30 minutes or as long as 4 hours. (If chilled longer, the dough will become discolored.)

◇ When you're ready to make your pie, preheat the oven to 400°F. Line the pie shell with a piece of parchment paper or aluminum foil, and fill it with pie weights, dry beans, or pennies to keep it from puffing up while baking. Bake until the crust is set, about 15 minutes. Remove the parchment or foil and let the crust stand on a cooling rack while you make the filling.

◇ To make the pie filling, reduce the oven temperature to 325°F, leaving the oven door cracked open to allow the oven to cool down more quickly. Place the walnuts on a baking sheet and toast them in the oven until they are fragrant and just a shade darker, 8 to 10 minutes. Warm the walnut oil in a large saucepan over medium-low heat and stir in the chocolate, stirring with a wire whisk just until the chocolate is beginning to melt. Remove the pan from the heat and continue stirring until the chocolate is completely melted. Whisk in the brown sugar, the corn syrup, and then the eggs, one at a time. Stir in the bourbon, vanilla, and salt.

◇ With a rolling pin, gently crush the toasted walnuts, then pile them into the partially baked pie crust. Pour the chocolate mixture over the walnuts. Bake until the center is slightly puffed and just beginning to crack around the edges, 50 to 60 minutes. Transfer the pie to a cooling rack and let it cool for at least 1 hour before cutting. Serve the pie at room temperature, garnished with lightly sweetened whipped cream, if desired.

Makes 8 servings

SHABBOS

"The idle man does not know what it is to enjoy rest."
—ALBERT EINSTEIN

For me, home cooking has always been as much about leisure as it is about work. Even when I cook for forty or fifty hours a week in a restaurant, I look forward to cooking at home.

Like everyone I know, I am pressed to accomplish more than I do, more than I can. Something in our culture, perhaps in the very fiber of our being, tells us to seize the day, to make hay while the sun shines. The brevity of life is always and everywhere apparent—in Andrew Marvell's immortal words, "But at my back I always hear / Time's winged chariot hurrying near."

Interestingly enough, when I actually stop to listen for the sound of that chariot, what I hear instead is the music of the spheres. Urgency falls away and all seems incredibly well. As so many of the sages have taught over the millennia, being fully present in any given moment can be completely liberating.

I think the sense of urgency that so many of us feel is often artificial, fabricated by promoters of products that would "save time" and afford us the imaginary leisure that their convenience products supposedly create. Certainly, a lot of bad food has been pushed off in the name of convenience, and rather than leisure, those "convenience foods" seem to provide a restless sort of dissatisfaction. I understand that people are busy. But if we're so damn busy, how is it that we have time to watch television for an average of something in the neighborhood of forty hours a week? And isn't it curious that, for millions of Americans, a good deal of those hours are spent watching people cook? How can you have time to watch the Food Network if you don't have time to cook?

Maybe people have more time than they think they do. Maybe what they lack is not so much time as it is skill. I would propose that being still and developing the patience and skill to produce a few good meals from scratch might solve a good number of this world's ills. What's more, cooking in and of itself is an activity that provides considerable pleasure for its practitioners, kind of like practicing yoga or swimming. We might engage in these activities with a result in mind— dinner, a clear mind, a healthy body—but the activity itself provides an opportunity to enter a zone where one can find something better than leisure. Cooking, when it's done well, by anyone who has taken time to learn the craft, can be a kind of spiritual practice.

In one of my favorite pictures of my mother, she is pregnant with me, sitting at the small Formica-topped table in the kitchen of her ground-floor apartment that was across the street from my grandparents' house. The light is streaming in from an eastern window, so I know it was morning. She has a pencil in one hand and, although my mother wrote poems and spent some time drawing, I can tell she is not working on either one of those things. I know exactly what she was working on because I saw her doing it hundreds of times with exactly the same awkward posture and the same concentrated look on her face. She was writing out a menu. She used to do it every week. She would write the menus for the dinners she was going to prepare that week, and from that list, she would derive her grocery list. It may have been part of her job as a homemaker, a form of work. But I think it was restful for her, too, a kind of practical meditation.

In his thoughtful book of essays, *Sabbath: Restoring the Sacred Rhythm of Rest*, Wayne Muller explores not only the sacred day of rest from the Ten Commandments, but also the whole notion of rest. "For six days you shall labor and do all your work. But the seventh day is a Sabbath to the Lord your God; you shall not do any work—you, or your son or your daughter, or your male or female slave, or your ox or your donkey, or any of your livestock, or the resident alien in your towns, so that your male and female slave may rest as well as you." What a groundbreaking idea this must have been in the ancient world when only the privileged were expected to take any sort of leisure.

The whole notion of Sabbath reminds us to pause, to take stock of what is at hand and to remember that every moment is a gift. It doesn't have to take all day—although it would be good, I suppose, if one was able to take a full day, once a week, to dwell on one's blessings. As Muller points out, observing the Sabbath might be possible in a less traditional way. We can find moments of Sabbath-like peace and joy in the midst of our everyday activities.

"Sabbath can . . . be a far-reaching, revolutionary tool for cultivating those precious human qualities that grow only in time," Muller says. Busyness, on the other hand, can be a kind of violence: "When we are moving faster and faster, every encounter, every detail inflates in importance, everything seems more urgent than it really is, and we react with sloppy desperation." Sabbath counteracts that violence with a dose of peace. Too busy to cook? Turn off the Food Network and open a cookbook.

In my own experience, I find a little dose of Sabbath in a twenty-minute walk. It can be a single deep breath, or it can be the ten minutes I spend hunched over the kitchen counter in a professional kitchen writing out a prep list. As soon as I stop focusing on what comes next and simply contemplate the now, taking the time to be fully present for a moment, then time opens up. Somehow, in the process of practicing a skill—like planning a menu, making a prep list, or especially cooking—I find rest. If I am deeply involved in the moment, fully present to the browning of butter around a fillet of sole, or right in tune with a spear of broccoli turning that bright shade of emerald green that tells me it's ready, then I'm in a state of grace.

Of course, any traditional observation of the Sabbath includes prohibitions on work. But for those of us who cook, whether professionally or for pleasure, practicing our craft can bring moments of unexpected peace, moments of rest or Shabbos, if you will, even in the midst of work. Right in the middle of all the activity involved in bringing food to the table—chopping, sautéing, stirring, folding, kneading, tasting—there are opportunities to revel in the activity at hand.

Sometimes, especially when I am performing a task I have done many times, I feel completely restful in the activity. Chopping an onion or kneading dough summons a subtle rhythm and charm that make me feel profoundly at ease. And when you have chopped an onion a thousand times, it can suddenly, inexplicably, become new again. Pure muscle memory is responsible for the activity, but the conscious mind steps in and observes it happening, and re-embraces the task, and a kind of divinity enters in. There is an old Zen koan that goes, "Before enlightenment, chop wood, haul water; after enlightenment, chop wood, haul water."

I can't say that cooking forces us to slow down and get in touch with what's happening in the present, but I will say that it can provide opportunities to do just that. Like any other craft, cooking affords those who do it a sense of satisfaction, serving as an antidote to the hectic pace of our workaday lives. What's more, having prepared a meal, the cook can usually find time and company to share a few blessed moments enjoying the fruits of her labor. It is, of course, in the eating, not in the cooking, that we find Sabbath in the biblical sense, but I have to say that sometimes cooking is more pleasurable than eating, even when the food turns out well. And I swear food tastes better, and leisure time feels more leisurely, when it involves something I cooked myself.

CHALLAH

The traditional festive bread served at a Jewish Sabbath dinner, challah is a sweet, tender, braided loaf enriched with eggs and oil. I'm not Jewish, but I started baking this bread in my early teens when I was captivated by a picture of it in a book. As I gradually came to understand its significance, I came to appreciate it more and more. The bread is designed to last for a couple of days, so any leftover is great the next day. It makes great sandwich bread and incredible French toast.

For the bread

  1½ cups warm (about 90°F) water

  1 tablespoon active dry yeast

  6½ to 7 cups bread flour, divided

  3 eggs

  ⅓ cup sugar

  ⅓ cup canola oil

  2 tablespoons kosher salt

For the egg wash

  1 egg

  1 tablespoon water

  1 tablespoon sugar

  2 tablespoons sesame seeds (optional)

◇ Pour the warm water into a large, warmed mixing bowl. Sprinkle the yeast over the water and stir until the yeast is dissolved. Whisk in 2 cups of the flour and allow the mixture to stand undisturbed for 30 minutes.

◇ Whisk the eggs, sugar, oil, and salt into the flour mixture. Whisk in 1 cup of the flour. Switching to a wooden spoon, stir in 2 more cups of flour, 1 cup at a time, stirring well between each addition. When the dough becomes too stiff to stir, work in enough of the remaining flour with your hands to form a fairly stiff dough.

◇ Turn the dough out onto a lightly floured surface and knead the dough, pressing it and folding it until it is smooth and elastic, sprinkling on additional flour to keep the dough from sticking to the counter.

◇ Clean out the bowl in which the dough was mixed and rub the inside of the bowl with the oil. Put the kneaded dough in the bowl and turn the dough over once so that the whole ball of dough is lightly coated with the oil. Cover the bowl with a damp, lint-free kitchen towel or with a piece of plastic wrap and put it in a warm place until the dough is doubled in size, about 1 hour.

◇ Line a baking sheet with parchment paper. Press the air out of the risen dough. Divide it in half and cut each half of the dough into 3 equal pieces. Shape each piece into a smooth ball; allow the dough balls to rest for 10 minutes. Roll the dough pieces, one at a time, into ropes about 12 inches long. Braid the ropes of dough into 2 neat loaves, tucking the loose ends under the ends, and put the loaves on the prepared baking sheet.

◇ Allow the loaves to rise until they are almost doubled, about 35 minutes. While the loaves are rising, preheat the oven to 350°F. Bake the risen loaves until they are well browned and baked through, about 40 minutes; they will sound hollow when tapped on the surface, and an instant-read thermometer should register 200°F.

◇ While the loaves are baking, whisk together the egg, water, and sugar, and when the loaves come out of the oven, brush them with the egg wash. Sprinkle the loaves with the sesame seeds, and return them to the oven to bake for 10 minutes more. Cool the loaves completely on a rack before slicing into them.

Makes 2 large loaves

BEST FRENCH TOAST

French cooks call this simple dish pain perdu, *or "lost bread," which is a sort of double entendre; the bread would otherwise be lost because it is stale, and the stale bread is "lost" because it is transformed into something new. My favorite French toast comes from leftover homemade challah, but day-old slices of a baguette work well, too.*

I egg
2 tablespoons brown sugar
I teaspoon vanilla extract
½ cup milk
Six ½-inch-thick slices day-old challah, or twelve ½-inch-thick
   slices day-old baguette
4 tablespoons unsalted butter
4 tablespoons powdered sugar

◇ Preheat a griddle or a cast-iron skillet over medium heat.

◇ In a wide, shallow bowl or a 9-inch baking dish, whisk together the egg, brown sugar, and vanilla, then whisk in the milk. Soak the sliced bread in this mixture, turning the slices over and pressing lightly once or twice for 1 minute or so to force them to soak up all the egg mixture.

◇ Melt the butter on the griddle or in the skillet and arrange the egg-soaked bread in a single layer in the melted butter. If any of the egg mixture remains in the baking dish (there won't be much), drizzle it over the surface of the bread. Cook until the undersides of the bread slices are well browned, about 3 minutes, then turn and cook until the other side is browned, about 2 minutes longer.

◇ Serve the toasts, 2 or 3 slices per serving, sprinkled with about 1 tablespoon of the powdered sugar over the top.

Makes 4 servings

INDEX